CAMBRIDGE LIBRARY COLLECTION

Books of enduring scholarly value

Classics

From the Renaissance to the nineteenth century, Latin and Greek were compulsory subjects in almost all European universities, and most early modern scholars published their research and conducted international correspondence in Latin. Latin had continued in use in Western Europe long after the fall of the Roman empire as the lingua franca of the educated classes and of law, diplomacy, religion and university teaching. The flight of Greek scholars to the West after the fall of Constantinople in 1453 gave impetus to the study of ancient Greek literature and the Greek New Testament. Eventually, just as nineteenth-century reforms of university curricula were beginning to erode this ascendancy, developments in textual criticism and linguistic analysis, and new ways of studying ancient societies, especially archaeology, led to renewed enthusiasm for the Classics. This collection offers works of criticism, interpretation and synthesis by the outstanding scholars of the nineteenth century.

Arundines Cami

Arundines Cami ('The Reeds of the Cam') is a collection of over 200 English rhymes, songs, poems, and hymns translated into Latin (and occasionally Greek) by a group of early Victorian Cambridge alumni. It was compiled and edited by Henry Drury (1812–1863), a graduate of Gonville and Caius College. A promising classical scholar, Drury left Cambridge in 1839 to embark on a career in the church, and became curate of Alderley, Gloucestershire. The following year, Drury and some friends conceived this anthology which includes the full text of selected English poems by authors including Tennyson, Shakespeare, Byron, Gray, Burns and Milton, accompanied by Latin translations. Drury dedicated the book, first published in 1841, to his *alma mater*. A total of six editions were published, the first five during Drury's lifetime, and the last in 1865, edited by H.J. Hodgson.

T0382543

Cambridge University Press has long been a pioneer in the reissuing of out-of-print titles from its own backlist, producing digital reprints of books that are still sought after by scholars and students but could not be reprinted economically using traditional technology. The Cambridge Library Collection extends this activity to a wider range of books which are still of importance to researchers and professionals, either for the source material they contain, or as landmarks in the history of their academic discipline.

Drawing from the world-renowned collections in the Cambridge University Library, and guided by the advice of experts in each subject area, Cambridge University Press is using state-of-the-art scanning machines in its own Printing House to capture the content of each book selected for inclusion. The files are processed to give a consistently clear, crisp image, and the books finished to the high quality standard for which the Press is recognised around the world. The latest print-on-demand technology ensures that the books will remain available indefinitely, and that orders for single or multiple copies can quickly be supplied.

The Cambridge Library Collection will bring back to life books of enduring scholarly value (including out-of-copyright works originally issued by other publishers) across a wide range of disciplines in the humanities and social sciences and in science and technology.

Arundines Cami

*Sive Musarum Cantabrigiensium
Lusus Canori*

EDITED BY HENRY DRURY

CAMBRIDGE
UNIVERSITY PRESS

CAMBRIDGE UNIVERSITY PRESS

Cambridge, New York, Melbourne, Madrid, Cape Town, Singapore,
São Paolo, Delhi, Dubai, Tokyo

Published in the United States of America by Cambridge University Press, New York

www.cambridge.org
Information on this title: www.cambridge.org/9781108012010

© in this compilation Cambridge University Press 2009

This edition first published 1841
This digitally printed version 2009

ISBN 978-1-108-01201-0 Paperback

PARS PRIMA.

ARUNDINES CAMI

SIVE

MUSARUM CANTABRIGIENSIUM

LUSUS CANORI

COLLEGIT ATQUE EDIDIT

HENRICUS DRURY, A.M.

Equitare in arundine longa.

CANTABRIGIÆ:

TYPIS ACADEMICIS EXCUSUS.

VENEUNT APUD J. ET J. J. DEIGHTON, CANTABRIGIÆ;
ET J. G. PARKER, LONDINI.

M.DCCC.XLI.

ALMAE . MATRI

ACADEMIAE . CANTABRIGIENSI.

HOS . ARVNDINVM . VOCALIVM . SVSVRROS.

GRATO . ANIMO.

D . D   D.

HENRICVS . DRVRY.

ARTIVM . MAGISTER.

LECTORI S.

Ne mireris, Lector erudite, quod in ævo rerum utilium magis sagaci, quam ornamentorum studioso, novos quosdam ' Musarum fœtus' ausim expromere, id accuratius edoceri fortasse non gravaberis.

Quum jam, ad sublimiora studia vocatus, ab Academia nostra discessissem, venit mihi in mentem, quæ calamo Græco aut Latino luseram, subsecivis horis in fasciculum unum colligere. Huc accessere quædam non invenustæ prolusiones eorum quibus familiarissime versatus sum; eaque omnia collata tandem et comparata, ita mihi arridebant, ut oculis viderer paternis tanquam filiolos meos intueri; intuens autem, mox cuperem oculos omnium hominum in eosdem convertere. Cæterum, his vixdum perpensis, prout plurima vires eundo acquirunt, quæ somniarer, aliis quibusdam Cantabrigiensibus impertitus sum, et paulatim auxilia in re audacissima supplicavi. Itaque brevi tempore nescio quæ Nasonum et Maronum et Poetarum Scenicorum scrinia non in manus meas fuerint effusa; imo, ne te morer, ea erat munificentia vatum et Latine et Attice scribentium, ut in seligendo magis quam colligendo summus labor constaret.

Inter has opes, plurimi faciebam quæcunque a Musis nostratibus Latine reddita acciperem, eademque diligenter excerpebam. Etenim experiendo cognovi animum lectoris hoc genus eo libentius adire, quo acrioris ingenii vis in interpretando postulatur ; quo plus exigitur calliditatis in electione ac constructione verborum ; quo exquisitior patet doctrinæ concinnitas in accommodando linguæ obsoletæ non sua ἰδιώματα.

Jam vero veniam dabit Censor criticus, si seriem atque juncturam operis levissimi facetam magis quam legitimam, meorum arbiter, mihi proposuero. Quippe meminerit idem, si

> Illecebris erat et grata novitate morandus
> Spectator,

tamen non me fefellisse

> ita vertere seria ludo,

quin in alteram partem libelli omnia sacra per se reverenter essent seposita atque distributa.

Utrum feliciter necne conati sumus monachorum hymnos rhythmicos imitari, judicent alii : unum id in hoc loco jure lamentamur, quod ista species carminum, tam casta, tam pulcra, tam plena exercitationis idoneæ, cum in ludis publicis, tum apud Academicos nostros,

penitus omissa videatur. Quis autem ignorat quam egregia sit hodie ad versiones sacras opportunitas, seu quis
illius ' Lyræ Apostolicæ' fila solicitet, sive circa dædalos
flores, ' Anni Christiani' fundantur vatum examina?

Neque huic procemio ante siparia tollantur, quam,
adjutoribus meis, quorum erit omnis laus, si quid suavius
aut elegantius in Anthologia nostra eniteat, maximas
gratias persolvam. Inque iis præsertim ἀκολακεύτως ag-
nosco quod ego debeo Francisco Hodgson, Collegii
Etonensis Præposito; quod eruditissimo Francisco
Wrangham, inter Brigantes Archidiacono: quod Baroni
Lyttelton, quantum titulis, tantum ingenio et doctrina
nobili; quod denique amicissimo meo Henrico Johanni
Hodgson, e collegio SS. Trinitatis socio, et ab ovo
usque ad mala strenuo præ omnibus auxiliatori.

Superest, ut pacem tuam impetrem, lector benevole,
si fortasse quædam mendose, quædam negligentius, inter
has nugas, prelo commissa offendas. Cujusvis est hominis errare: quin et noster Vincentius Bourne (cui
Romanum fidicinem nunc temporis parem exploravi ne-
minem) ipse aliquoties peccat, et versus incomposito
pede currentes patitur. Spero autem te facilius mihi
obtemperaturum, si intellexeris, editorem tuum, neque
inter silvas Academi, neque propter susurrantes Ilissi ripas,
sed in rure reducto, procul ab amicis, procul a libris,

procul a doctissimorum colloquio, solum et tacitum et aliquando tristissimum, hos labores suos in lucem protulisse.

Tibi vero, Alma Mater 'lepidum novum libellum', qualiscunque sit, dono ac dedico. Tu, pro eo ac meretur, aut abjicies aut—si me amas, amplecteris. Tui gratam memoriam vel absens persequar. Quare fac me diligas, et dignitati meæ suffrageris.

Dabam apud GENISTARUM VILLAM.
D. xiii. Kal. *Aprilis.* $\overline{MD}$. $\overline{CCC}$. $\overline{XLI}$.

Arundinibus Contulerunt.

SAMUEL BUTLER, S.T.P. nuper Episcopus Lichfieldensis	S. B.
LORD LYTTELTON, A.M.	L.
LORD JOHN MANNERS, A.M.	J. M.
RICHARD PORSON, A.M.	R. P.
FRANCIS HODGSON, S.T.B. Etonæ Præpositus	F. H.
FRANCIS WRANGHAM, A.M. Inter Brigantes Archidiaconus.	F. W.
EDWARD CRAVEN HAWTREY, S.T.P. Scholæ Etonensis Archididascalus	E. C. H.
HENRY JOSEPH THOMAS DRURY, A.M. Scholæ Harroviensis nuper Subdidascalus..........................	H. J. T. D.
BENJAMIN HALL KENNEDY, S.T.P. Scholæ Salopiensis Archididascalus	B. H. K.
JOHN HEYRICK MACAULAY, A.M. Scholæ Reptonensis nuper Archididascalus.	J. H. M.[1]
JOHN HERMAN MERIVALE, A.M.	J. H. M.
JOHN NORBURY e Collegio Etonensi olim Socius......	J. N.
GEORGE CALDWELL, A.M. Collegii IESU Socius......	G. C.
HENRY ARTHUR HALLAM, A.M.	H. H.
WILLIAM JAMES LAW, A.M.	W. J. L.
CHARLES MERIVALE, S.T.B. Collegii D. Johannis Socius.	C. M.
JAMES HILDYARD, A.M. Collegii Christi Socius.......	J. H.
GEORGE KENNEDY, A.M. Collegii D. Johannis Socius	G. K.
JOHN WILLIAM DONALDSON, A.M. Collegii SS. Trinitatis Socius	J. W. D.
ALEXANDER FREDERICK MERIVALE, A.M. Collegii SS. Trinitatis Socius...............................	A. F. M.
WILLIAM GILSON HUMPHRY, A.M. Collegii SS. Trinitatis Socius	W. G. H.
GEORGE CURREY, A.M. Collegii D. Johannis Socius...	G. C.
HENRY JOHN HODGSON, A.M. Collegii SS. Trinitatis Socius	H. I. H.
BENJAMIN HEATH DRURY, A.B. e Magistris Scholæ Harroviensis.	B. H. D.
ALEXANDER BERESFORD HOPE, A.B....................	A. B. H.
HENRY DRURY, A.M	H. D.

[1] Gray's Elegy.

INDEX CARMINUM.

PARS PRIMA.

PARS SECUNDA.

ARUNDINES CAMI.

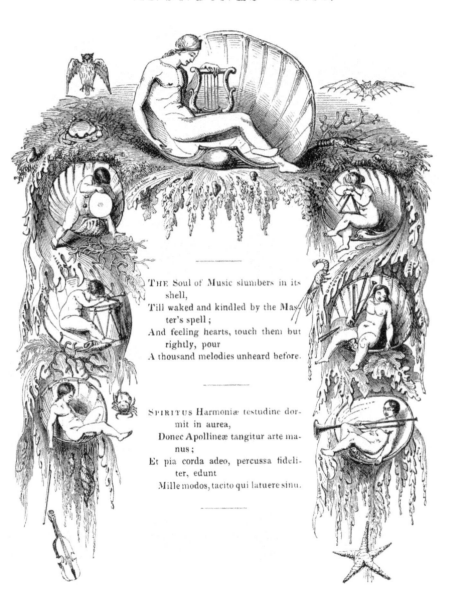

THE Soul of Music slumbers in its
    shell,
Till waked and kindled by the Mas-
    ter's spell ;
And feeling hearts, touch them but
    rightly, pour
A thousand melodies unheard before.

SPIRITUS Harmoniæ testudine dor-
    mit in aurea,
    Donec Apollineæ tangitur arte ma-
      nus ;
Et pia corda adeo, percussa fideli-
      ter, edunt
    Mille modos, tacito qui latuere sinu.

A SIXPENNY SONG.

Sing a song of sixpence,
  A pocket full of rye:
Four and twenty blackbirds
  Baked in a pie.
When the pie was opened,
  The birds began to sing;
Was not that a dainty dish
  To set before the King?

The King was in the parlour
  Counting out his money;
The Queen was in the kitchen
  Eating bread and honey;
The Maid was in the garden
  Hanging out the clothes;
Down came a blackbird
  And perched upon her nose.

GAMMER GURTON.

INSCRIPTION ON AN ANTIQUE RING.

I'll heare thy voice of melodie
  In whispers of the summerre air;
I'll see the brightnesse of thine eye
  In the blue eveninge's shininge starre;
In moonlighte beames thy puritie;
And look on heavenne, to look on thee!

CROLY.

CARMEN DENARIUM.

INCIPE cui titulo ' Denarius,' incipe cantum !
  Huic tumido loculo massa secalis inest :
Sex quater in patina merularum corpora, crustum
  Queis superimpositum pista farina fuit,
Procubuere simul : sed quando adaperta farina est,
  Concordes merulis insonuere modi :
Mirum opus harmoniæ !—nonne inter fercula posset
  Hæc vel regificæ lanx placuisse gulæ ?

Rex erat in camera, numerans sibi pondera nummi,
  Pondera plebeio non numeranda viro :
Mel mandit panemque morans Regina culina ;
  Dulcia plebeia non comedenda nuru.
Ad solem vestes siccans Ancilla per hortum
  Ibat ; et expansas aere funis habet ;
Quum merula, affini descendens arbore, nasum
  Ancillæ insiluit seque ibi constituit.

F. H.

INSCRIPTUM IN ANNULO ANTIQUO.

  VERNI canoris in Noti suspiriis
  Cœleste vocis audiam melos tuæ ;
  Oculi videbo fulgidi purum jubar
  Non infidelis Hesperi sub ignibus :
  Formosa mentem Luna depinget tuam ;
  Teque intuebor, intuens cœli vias.

H. D.

ODE TO ADVERSITY.

Daughter of Jove, relentless power,
Thou tamer of the human breast,
Whose iron scourge and torturing hour
The bad affright, afflict the best !
Bound in thy adamantine chain,
The proud are taught to taste of pain,
And purple tyrants vainly groan
With pangs unfelt before, unpitied and alone.

When first thy Sire to send on earth
Virtue, his darling child, designed,
To thee he gave the heavenly birth,
And bad to form her infant mind.
Stern rugged Nurse ! thy rigid lore
With patience many a year she bore ;
What sorrow was thou bad'st her know,
And from her own she learned to melt at others' woe.

Gray.

IN CALAMITATEM.

Quæ sævo domitos imperio regis
Mortales, superi nata Jovis Dea,
    Dira non sine pœna et
      Flagris improba ferreis

Pertentans homines; unde adamantinis
Sub vinclis trepidum comprimitur Nefas,
    Angunturque malorum
      Seris pectora luctibus,

Nec puri sceleris non animi dolent;
Te reges dominam purpurei novam,
    Deserti sociorum,
      Te vano gemitu tremunt.

Cum lectam generi mittere filiam
Humano voluit cœlicolum Pater
    Virtutem, tibi diam
      Commisit sobolem Deus,

Ut prudens teneræ pectora fingeres.
Ah quanta rigidam te patientia,
    Nutrix aspera, longis
      Virtus temporibus tulit!

Sensit, qua miseris fracta doloribus
Mens cura gemeret: sensit, et haud suo,
    Te perdocta magistra,
      Luctu tangitur invicem.

                        L.

SANDY'S GHOST.

THE Moon had climbed the highest hill
  Which rises o'er the source of Dee,
And from the eastern summit shed
  Her silvery light o'er tower and tree;

When Mary laid her down to sleep,
  Her thoughts on Sandy far at sea,
When low and soft a voice she heard
  Say—'Mary, weep no more for me.'

She from her pillow gently raised
  Her head, to see who there might be;
She saw young Sandy shivering stand,
  With visage pale and hollow e'e.

'O Maiden dear, cold is my clay,
  'It lies beneath a stormy sea;
'Far far from thee I sleep in death,
  'So, Mary,—weep no more for me.

'O Maiden dear, thyself prepare,
  'We soon shall meet upon that shore
'Where love is free from doubt and care,
  'And we shall meet to part no more.'

Loud crowed the cock; the Shadow fled;
  No more of Sandy could she see;
But soft the parting Spirit said—
  'Sweet Mary, weep no more for me.'

OLD BALLAD.

ALEXIS UMBRA.

QUOD perlucentis spectat cunabula Devæ,
  Luna super summum fulserat alba jugum ;
Argentique faces Eoi a vertice cœli
  Sparserat in sylvas turrigerasque domos.

In lecto composta suum jam Phyllis Alexin
  Visa erat in somnis per freta longa sequi,
Quum pressum irrepsit murmur—' Mea Phylli, quiescas ;
  ' Desine torqueri quod tuus absit Amor.'

Sustulit a mœsto tremulum caput illa cubili,
  Quæsitum in thalamo quis sit et unde suo ;
Et stare algentem pede lecti vidit Alexin,
  Exsangui vultu luminibusque cavis.

' Sternor ego exanimis, vita O mihi carior ipsa,
  ' Intempestivo pulvis et ossa mari ;
' Te procul accumbo morti—mea Phylli, quiescas ;
  ' Nequicquam quereris, quod tuus absit Amor.

' Suave meum, non longa mora est—modo mollia tangas
  ' Numina—quin sacra congrediamur humo ;
' Qua manet inconcussa Fides, secura laborum ;
  ' Qua nunquam amplexu diripiere meo.'

Fortiter increpuit gallus : vaga fugit Imago :
  Vanuit ex oculis quod fuit omne viri,
Dixitque abscedens tenere—' Mea Phylli, quiescas ;
  ' Desine torqueri quod tuus absit Amor.'

                                        H. D.

TAFFY WAS A WELSHMAN.

Taffy was a Welshman, and Taffy was a thief,
Taffy came to my house and stole a bit of beef;
I went to Taffy's house; Taffy wasn't at home;
Taffy came to my house and stole a marrow bone.
I went to Taffy's house; Taffy was in bed;
I took up the marrow bone and beat about his head.

GAMMER GURTON.

MAD TOM.

I am mad Tom, behold me!
My senses are gone from me;
  I'm mad, I'm sure,
  I'm past all cure,
And Bedlam scarce can hold me.

I'll climb yon lofty mountain,
And there I'll fight the gypsies;
  I'll play at bowls
  With the sun and moon,
And beat them both to eclipses.

I'm wiser than Apollo;
For while he lay a sleeping,
  I saw the stars
  At mortal jars,
While Vulcan was a weeping.

ANON.

QUOD FECERIM CUM TAFFIO.

TAFFIUS in Cimbris natus, fur Taffius idem;
Accessitque fores nostras, carnemque bovillam
Surripuit: frustra pulsabam limina Taffi,
Ille aberat—rediitque meos, velut ante, penates
Osque medullosum malus abstulit. Ipse reversus
Invenisse domi furem lectoque reclinem
Lætor, et osse caput rapto sine judice cædo.

F. H.

THOMAS DEMENS.

ECCE, furens Thomas! Sensus fugere, nec ullam
    Suggerit insano cura medentis opem;
Distrahor, accendor flammis—quid ferrea possunt
    Claustra, quid Anticyræ jugera tota mihi?

Impiger adversi scandam juga devia montis,
    Atque Ægyptiaco cum grege bella geram;
Ire pilis lusum cum Luna et Sole parabor,
    Condiderit nitidum donec uterque latus.

Non quenquam fugio vel Apolline doctior ipso;
    In roseo nam dum dormiit ille toro,
Astra inter niveas vidi pugnantia nubes,
    Vulcani in fuscis imbre madente genis.

Ω.

I'D BE A BUTTERFLY.

I'D be a Butterfly born in a bower,
  Where roses and lilies and violets meet;
Roving for ever from flower to flower,
  And kissing all buds that are pretty and sweet!
I'd never languish for wealth or for power;
  I'd never sigh to see slaves at my feet:
I'd be a Butterfly born in a bower,
  Kissing all buds that are pretty and sweet.

O could I pilfer the wand of a fairy,
  I'd have a pair of those beautiful wings:
Their summer-day's ramble is sportive and airy,
  They sleep in a rose when the nightingale sings.
Those, who have wealth, must be watchful and wary;
  Power, alas! nought but misery brings!
I'd be a Butterfly sportive and airy,
  Rock'd in a rose when the nightingale sings!

What, though you tell me each gay little rover
  Shrinks from the breath of the first autumn day!
Sure it is better, when summer is over,
  To die when all fair things are fading away.
Some in life's winter may toil to discover
  Means of procuring a weary delay—
I'd be a Butterfly; living a rover,
  Dying when fair things are fading away!

HAYNES BAYLEY.

AH! SIM PAPILIO.

A<small>H</small>! sim Papilio natus in flosculo,
  Rosæ ubi liliaque et violæ halent;
Floribus advolans, avolans, osculo
  Gemmulas tangens, quæ suave olent!
Sceptra et opes ego neutiquam postulo,
  Nolo ego ad pedes qui se volutent:—
Ah! sim Papilio natus in flosculo,
  Osculans gemmas quæ suave olent!

Magicam si possem virgam furari,
  Alas has pulcras aptem mi, eheu!
Æstivis actis diebus in aëre,
  Rosa cubant Philomelæ cantu.
Opes quid afferunt?—curas, somnum rare:
  Sceptra nil præter ærumnas, eheu!
Ah! sim Papilio, die volans aëre,
  Rosa cubans Philomelæ cantu!

Quemque horum vagulum dicis horrore
  Frigora autumni ferire suo:
Æstas quando abiit, mallem ego mori,
  Omni quod dulce est cadente pulcro.
Brumæ qui cupiunt captent labore
  Gaudia, et moras breves trahunto—
Ah! sim Papilio: vivam in errore,
  Concidamque omni cadente pulcro!

F W

THE LOTOS EATERS.

Branches they bore of that enchanted stem,
Laden with flower and fruit, whereof they gave
To each: but whoso did receive of them
And taste, to him the gushing of the wave
Far far away did seem to mourn and rave
On alien shores; and if his fellow spake,
His voice was thin, as voices from the grave;
And deep-asleep he seemed, yet all awake;
And music in his ears his beating heart did wake.

They sat them down upon the yellow sand,
Between the sun and moon, upon the shore;
And sweet it was to dream of Father-land,
And wife and child and slave; but evermore
Most weary seemed the sea, weary the oar,
Weary the wandering fields of barren foam.
Then some one said, ' We will return no more;'—
And all at once they sang, ' Our island home
' Is far beyond the wave; we will no longer roam.'

TENNYSON.

BANDY LEGS.

As I was a going to sell my eggs,
I met a man with bandy legs,
Bandy legs and crooked toes:—
I tripped up his heels, and he fell on his nose.

GAMMER GURTON.

LOTOPHAGI.

QUINETIAM magica ramos de stirpe ferebant,
Floribus et fructu gravidos, et dulcia cuique
Dona dabant: quorum succo semel ore recepto,
Visa procul longis incassum anfractibus unda
Mugire increpitans, et non sua litora plangi:
Et tenuis, sociorum aliquis si forte locutus,
Stridere vox, Lemurum velut imbecilla querela:
Et licet insomnis, somno cogi inque pediri
Omnis; et auditis tremulo modulamine fibris,
Suave sub arguto geminari pectore murmur.
Consedere omnes ad flavæ litus arenæ,
In medio Solis radios Lunæque tuentes:
Et patriæ dulcis, sobolisque irrepit imago
Mentibus, et veteris procul oblectamina vitæ:
Tædia mox pelagus, remi quoque tædia visi
Ingerere et spumæ sterilis longissimus æstus;
Atque aliquis tandem—' non amplius ibimus,' inquit:
Continuoque omnes—' longe mare clauditur ultra
' Insula, nostra domus: non amplius ibimus'—omnes.

C. M.

VARO QUOD ACCIDIT.

IBAM forte forum vendendis impiger ovis;
  Obvius incurvis vir mihi fit pedibus,
Cruribus et varis: mihi supplantare misellum
  Sors erat; in nares incidit ille solo.

F. H.

THE BLIND MAN'S BRIDE.

WHEN first, beloved, in vanished hours,
 The Blind Man sought thy hand to gain,
They said thy cheek was bright as flowers
 New freshened by the summer's rain.
The beauty which made them rejoice
 My darkened eyes might never see,
But well I knew thy gentle voice,
 And that was all in all to me.

At length, as years rolled swiftly on,
 They talked to me of Time's decay,
Of roses from thy soft cheek gone,
 Of ebon tresses turned to grey.
I heard them; but I heeded not;
 The withering change I could not see;
Thy voice still cheered my darkened lot,
 And that was all in all to me.

And still, beloved, till life grows cold,
 We'll wander 'neath the genial sky,
And only know that we are old
 By counting happy hours gone by.
Thy cheek may lose its blushing hue,
 Thy brow less beautiful may be;
But oh the voice, which first I knew,
 Still keeps the same sweet tone to me!

MRS NORTON.

CÆCUS AD UXOREM.

TEMPORE præterito cum te, dilecta, petebam
  Conjugio mecum jungere cæcus ego;
Ipsa (susurrabant) ibas pulcherrima rerum,
  Flore prior verna qui recreatur aqua.
Quæ tam grata aliis, qui te videre, venustas
  Fulserit—heu! oculis abditur illa meis.
Sed blanda est auri tua vox bene cognita nostræ:
  Id fuit e votis omnibus omne mihi.

At quia labuntur reduces velociter anni,
  Jam formæ memorant plurima damna tuæ;
Quod nigri albescant rugosa in fronte capilli,
  Quod rosa sit teneris deperitura genis.
Inscius audivi: nec sunt mihi talia curæ;
  Effugiant veneres, non ego testis ero:
Mulsit adhuc mea me vocis dulcedine conjux:
  Id fuit e votis omnibus omne mihi.

Sic, dilecta, una sub cœlo errabimus almo,
  Dum brevis in nostro pectore vita calet;
Et, nisi felices quando numerabimus horas,
  Immemores erimus nos simul esse senes.
Quod si non vultu maneat color ille rosarum,
  Frons etiam uxori sit minus alba meæ;
Vox tua suaviloqua me cepit imagine primum;
  Vox tua dat liquidum, quod dedit ante, melos.

                                H. I. H.

THE OLD GENTLEMAN OF TOBAGO.

THERE was an old man of Tobago,
Who lived on rice gruel and sago;
　　Till much to his bliss
　　His physician said this—
'To a leg, Sir, of mutton you may go.'

GAMMER GURTON.

SENEX TOBAGENSIS.

JAMDUDUM senior quidam de rure Tobagus
  Invito madidas carpserat ore dapes:
Sed Medicus tandem, non injucunda locutus,
  ' Assæ,' dixit, ' oves sint tibi cœna, senex.'

ΓΕΡΩΝ τις, οἰκῶν τοὺς Τοβαγῴους μύχους,
ἐδειπνοποιεῖ σαγινὴν δηρὸν τροφήν·
τέλος δ' ἰατρος εἶπε, χαρμονὴν κλύειν,
φάγοις ἂν ἤδη πρόβατον, ὦ μάκαρ γέρον.

J'AI entendu parler d'un viellard de Tobag,
Qui ne mangea longtems que du ris et du sague:
Mais enfin le Medecin lui dit ces mots,
' Allez-vous-en, mon ami, au gigot.'

UN vecchio, che visse nel Tobago,
Da lungo tempo inghiottiva sago;
Ma infin il Medico disse un grato detto;
' Mangiar carne arrostita io vi permetto.'

W. J. D.

CUPID AND CAMPASPE.

Cupid and my Campaspe play'd
At cardes for kisses; Cupid pay'd:
He stakes his quiver, bow and arrows,
His mother's doves, and teame of sparrows;
Loses them too; then down he throws
The coral of his lippe, the rose
Growing on's cheek (but none knows how);
With these the crystal of his browe,
And then the dimple of his chinne;
All these did my Campaspe winne.
At last he set her both his eyes;
She won, and Cupid blind did rise.

    O Love! has she done this to thee?
    What shall alas! become of mee?

                    LELY.

ADIEU, ADIEU! MY NATIVE SHORE.

" Adieu, adieu! my native shore
    Fades o'er the waters blue;
The Night-winds sigh, the breakers roar,
    And shrieks the wild sea-mew.
Yon Sun that sets upon the sea
    We follow in his flight;
Farewell awhile to him and thee,
    My native Land—Good Night!

AMOR ET CAMPASPE.

LUDEBANT simul alea Cupido et
Campaspe mea pignore osculorum :
Hæc rapto fruitur ; sed ille postis
Arcuque et pharetra, suis sagittis,
Materno pare passerum et columbis,
Jactu perdit et illa ; perditisque,
Promit curalium labri, rosamque
Miris ingenitam modis genarum ;
His et marmora frontis et latentem
Addit purpureo sub ore risum ;
Quæcumque opposuit, rapit puella.
Certat in geminos dehinc ocellos,
Exsurgitque oculis minor Cupido.
   O factum male vel Deo ! sed in me
   Mortali misero ah quid est futurum ?

                       G. C.

VALE BRITANNIA.

" TERRA paterna vale ! vitrei trans marmora ponti
   Labitur ex oculis terra paterna meis :
Flamina rauca sonant, reboant in litora fluctus,
   Spumea cum strepitu nubila mergus arat.
Hunc, vespertinis sol qui se condit in undis,
   Urgemus celeri subsequimurque fuga.
Paulum igitur valeas tu, sol pulcherrime—tuque
   Terra, mihi longum destituenda, vale !

" A few short hours and He will rise
  To give the morrow birth;
And I shall hail the main and skies,
  But not my mother earth.
Deserted is my own good hall,
  Its hearth is desolate;
Wild weeds are gathering on the wall;
  My dog howls at the gate.

" Come hither, hither, my little page!
  Why dost thou weep and wail?
Or dost thou dread the billow's rage,
  Or tremble at the gale?
But dash the tear-drop from thine eye;
  Our ship is swift and strong:
Our fleetest falcon scarce can fly
  More merrily along."

' Let winds be shrill, let waves roll high,
  I fear not wave nor wind:
Yet marvel not, Sir Childe, that I
  Am sorrowful in mind;
For I have from my father gone,
  A mother whom I love,
And have no friend, save these alone,
  But thee—and one above.

" Efferet Eoo mox se redivivus ab æstu
   Phœbus, et incipiet jam novus ire dies ;
Tum mare conspiciam et cœli convexa—paterni
   Sed non sunt iterum regna videnda soli.
Stat deserta domus ; patrum silet aula meorum ;
   Nec vetus est solito fervidus igne focus ;
Quin steriles herbæ dominantur pariete in ipso,
   Et canis occlusas ejulat ante fores.

" Huc, puer, huc venias !—venias, positoque dolore,
   Mœrendi quæ sit jam tibi causa refer.
Anne reformidas malesani turbinis iram,
   Anne times nimiis ne furat unda minis?
Pone metus, stantemque oculis i comprime guttam ;
   Firma per æquoreas hæc ratis ibit aquas ;
Nec, qui perspicuum rapidis secat æthera pennis,
   Accipiter cursu liberiore volat."

' Sæviat ira Noti, montes volvantur aquarum,
   Me nec aquæ tumidæ nec movet ira Noti.
Ne mirere tamen cura quod vexer, et ægri
   Quod subito luctus pectora nostra premant :
Nempe abiens carumque patrem matremque reliqui ;
   Omnibus abreptis tu mihi solus ades,
Tuque—Deusque manet—mihi tu nunc unus amicus ;
   Tu pro matre mihi, pro patre solus eris.

' My father bless'd me fervently,
    Yet did not much complain ;
But sorely will my mother sigh
    Till I come back again.'—
" Enough, enough, my little lad !
    Such tears become thine eye ;
If I thy guileless bosom had,
    Mine own would not be dry.

" Come hither, hither, my staunch yeoman,
    Why dost thou look so pale ?
Or dost thou dread a French foeman ?
    Or shiver at the gale ?"—
' Deem'st thou I tremble for my life ?
    Sir Childe, I'm not so weak ;
But thinking on an absent wife
    Will blanch a faithful cheek.

' My spouse and boys dwell near thy hall,
    Along the bordering lake,
And when they on their father call,
    What answer shall she make ?'—
" Enough, enough, my yeoman good,
    Thy grief let none gainsay ;
But I, who am of lighter mood,
    Will laugh to flee away.

' Tum mihi, (nam memini) pater est bona multa precatus,
  Pressa sed in forti est vana querela sinu.
At graviter puerum mater lugebit ademptum,
  Dum reduci gressu tecta paterna petam.'
" Causa satis justa est : ne sit flevisse pudori ;
  Non oculos fletus dedecet iste tuos ;
Quippe foret pariter si mens mihi criminis expers,
  Illa tuo pariter tacta dolore foret.

" Huc ades, O domini custos, fortissime miles,
  Dic age, cur tristi pallor in ore sedet ?
Scilicet id metuis ne nobis irruat hostis
  Gallicus ? an venti verbera sæva tremis ?"—
' Anne putas mortem causam satis esse timoris ?
  Non ita sum mollis, non ita triste mori est.
At deserta dolet quia, rapto conjuge, conjux,
  Exsulat a fidis purpura missa genis.

' Nempe uxor puerique, tui prope limina tecti,
  Litus habent vitrei, pignora cara, lacus :
Et cum sæpe pia me poscent voce parentem,
  Responsum pueris quod dabit illa suis ?'
" Et tibi causa satis—ne quis contemnat amorem,
  Nec tibi non æquum sic doluisse putet :
Ille, nec invideo, doleat, cui causa dolendi,—
  Læta tamen cum mens est mihi, læta fuga est.

" For who would trust the seeming sighs
   Of wife or paramour?
Fresh feres will dry the bright blue eyes
   We late saw streaming o'er.
For pleasures past I do not grieve,
   Nor perils gathering near;
My greatest grief is that I leave
   No thing that claims a tear.

" And now I'm in the world alone,
   Upon the wide, wide sea:
But why should I for others groan,
   When none will sigh for me?
Perchance my dog will whine in vain,
   Till fed by stranger hands;
But long ere I come back again
   He'd tear me where he stands.

" With thee, my bark, I'll swiftly go
   Athwart the foaming brine;
Nor care what land thou bear'st me to,
   So not again to mine.
Welcome, welcome, ye dark blue waves!
   And when you fail my sight,
Welcome, ye deserts, and ye caves!
   My native Land—Good Night!"

                      BYRON.

" Crederet infidæ, quamvis suspiret, amicæ
 Ecquis? habet proprios femina quæque dolos.
Cæruleos novus ignis erit qui siccet ocellos;
 Ridebunt, lacrymis quæ maduere, genæ.
Me neque præteritos lusus meminisse pigebit,
 Nec metuo in dubia quæ metuenda via:
At quia nil carum, nil post me dulce relinquo,
 Nil dignum lacrymis, hoc, mihi crede, dolet.

" Jam toto vagus orbe feror, peregrinus et exsul,
 Et circumfusum trans mare solus eo;
At, licet externas hospes sim missus in oras,
 Cum doleat nemo, cur miser ipse gemam?
In breve fors ululet tempus canis, altera donec
 Dextra cibum dederit, foverit alter amor;
Ante tamen multo quam tecta paterna revisam,
 Me dominum, priscum me laceraret herum.

" Te duce, remigio vectus, mea cymba, citato,
 Trajiciam salsi spumea regna maris:
Te duce, terrarum visam nova littora, promptus
 Quodlibet, id patrium ni sit, adire solum.
Cæruleæ salvete undæ, tenebræque profundi,—
 Cumque oculos visus deserat iste meos,
Vos nemora et solæ pariter salvete cavernæ;
 Nox cœlo properat: terra paterna, vale !"

J. H.

Brevity is the Soul of Wit.

SHAKESPEARE.

Si placeat Brevitas, hoc breve Carmen habe.

J. N.

THE PARENTS' WARNING.

THREE children sliding on the ice
    All on a summer's day,
As it fell out, they all fell in,—
    The rest they ran away.

Now had these children been at school,
    Sliding upon dry ground,
Ten thousand pounds to one penny
    They had not all been drowned.

You parents that have children dear,
    And eke you that have none,
If you will have them safe abroad,
    Pray keep them safe at home.
                    GAMMER GURTON.

PARENTES ADMONITI.

TRES ubi per glaciem pueri (nam incanduit æstas)
   Dirigerent celeres impavidosque pedes;
Accidit, inciderent ut in undas ocyus omnes;
   Vertitur in tutam cætera turba fugam.

Hos schola si pueros sua detinuisset et arens
   Jussisset pedibus pervolitare solum;
Pignoribus certem magnis tua parvula contra,
   Non omnes illos ira vorasset aquæ.

Vos quibus accessit proles dilecta, parentes;
   Vos etiam nullum est queis puerile genus;
Tutos esse foris vestros si vultis ephebos—
   O precor incolumes hos retinete domi!

F. H.

ALTERA VERSIO.

ΚΡΥΣΑΛΛΟΠΗΚΤΟΥΣ τρίπτυχοι κόροι ῥοὰς
῾Ωρᾳ θέρους ψαίροντες εὐτάρσοις ποσὶ,
Διναῖς ἔπιπτον, οἷα δὴ πίπτειν φιλεῖ,
῞Απαντες· εἶτ᾽ ἔφευγον οἱ λελειμμένοι.
῎Αλλ᾽ εἴπερ ἦσαν ἐγκεκλεισμένοι μοχλοῖς,
῍Η ποσὶν ὀλισθάνοντες ἐν ξηρῷ πέδῳ,
Χρυσῶν ἂν ἠθέλησα περιδόσθαι σταθμῶν,
Εἰ μὴ μέρος τι τῶν νέων ἐσώζετο.
῎Αλλ᾽ ὦ τοκεῖς, ὅσοις μὲν ὄντα τυγχάνει,
῞Οσοις δὲ μὴ, βλαστήματ᾽ εὐτέκνου σπορᾶς,
῍Ην εὐτυχεῖς εὔχησθε τὰς θύραζ᾽ ὁδοὺς
Τοῖς παισὶν, εὖ σφᾶς ἐν δόμοις φυλάσσετε.

R. P.

THE PLEDGE.

DRINK to me only with thine eyes,
    And I will pledge with mine;
Or leave a kiss within the cup,
    And I'll not ask for wine.
The thirst, that from the soul doth spring,
    Doth ask a draught divine;
But might I from Jove's nectar sip,
    I'd change it not for thine.

BEN JONSON.

PILLYCOCK.

OLD Pillycock sat on a grassy hill,
And if he's not gone, he sits there still.

GAMMER GURTON.

THE MARKS OF LOVE.

COME here, fond youth, whoe'er thou be,
That boast'st to love as well as me,
And if thy breast have felt so wide a wound,
    Come hither, and thy flame approve;
    I'll teach thee what it is to love,
And by what marks true passion may be found.

    It is to be all bathed in tears,
    To live upon a smile for years,
To lie whole ages at a beauty's feet,
    To kneel, to languish, to implore,
    And still, though she disdain, adore.
It is to do all this, and think thy sufferings sweet.

PROPINATIO.

Luminibus solis oro mihi, vita, propines;
  Luminibus reddam mox ego, crede, vices:
Aut tantum admoto cyathum mihi tinge labello,
  Et desiderium fugerit omne meri.
Scilicet, ex anima quæ fervida nascitur ima,
  Non nisi divino est fonte levanda Sitis.
Ast ego, donentur mihi si Jovis ipsa, recusem
  Pocula—sunt labris illa secunda tuis.

G. K.

PILLICOCCIUS.

Lacerpicifero jugo sedebat,
  Et si non abeat, diu sedebit,
  Spes ille ultima Pillicocciorum.

H. D.

INDICIA AMORIS.

Ferre parem nostris qui te, puer, ignibus ignem
  Jactas; si caleat quis tamen igne pari;
Infelix tua vota refer: referam ipse vicissim,
  Quid sit Amor, pateat qualibus ille notis.

Est, unum in totos risum depascier annos:
  Est, solvi in lacrymas, fundere vota, preces:
Ante pedes semper volvi et languere puellæ;
  Si fugit illa, sequi: sic cupere usque sequi.

It is to gaze upon her eyes
With eager joy and fond surprize,
Yet temper'd with such chaste and awful fear,
As wretches feel who wait their doom ;
Nor must one ruder thought presume,
Though but in whispers breathed, to meet her ear.

It is to hope, though hope were lost,
Though heaven and earth thy wishes cross'd :
Though she were bright as sainted queens above,
And thou the least and meanest swain
That folds his flock upon the plain,
Yet if thou darest not hope, thou dost not love.

It is to quench thy joy in tears,
To nurse strange thoughts and groundless fears :
If pangs of jealousy thou hast not proved,
Though she were fonder and more true
Than any nymph old poets drew,
O never dream again that thou hast loved.

If, when the darling maid is gone,
Thou dost not seek to be alone,
Rapt in a pleasing trance of tender woe ;
And muse and fold thy languid arms,
Feeding thy fancy on her charms,
Thou dost not love—for love is nourish'd so.

Est, in virgineis hærere ardenter ocellis ;

    Pectora dum cohibet, ceu peritura, timor,

Ne qua forte procax vel ab imo corde susurrus

    Auriculas stringat, commaculetque genas.

Est, spe dimissa non desperare ; resistant

    Si votis homines, si Deus ipse, tuis :

Illa licet Venerem superet, tuque infimus Ægon,

    Ni te spes foveat—non tibi notus Amor.

Est, lacrymas inter gaudere et gaudia luctu

    Miscere ; est, pacta contremere usque fide :

Namque licet casta sit castior illa Diana,

    Ni sic horrueris—non tibi notus Amor.

Dumque absit, ni percupias tecum esse, viasque

    Sæpius ambiguas incomitatus eas ;

Nescio quid tenerum meditans et totus in illo,

    Quicquid id est, raptus—non tibi notus Amor.

If any hopes thy bosom share
But those which Love has planted there,
Or any cares but his thy breast enthral,
   Thou never yet his power hast known:
   Love sits on a despotic throne,
And reigns a tyrant, if he reigns at all.

   Now if thou art so lost a thing,
   Hither thy tender sorrows bring,
And prove whose patience longest can endure:
   We'll strive whose fancy shall be tost
   In dreams of fondest passion most—
For if thou thus hast loved, oh never hope a cure!
BARBAULD.

LITTLE JACK HORNER.

LITTLE Jack Horner
Sat in a corner
   Eating a Christmas pie:
He put in his thumb
And pulled out a plum,
   And cried, ' What a good boy am I !'
GAMMER GURTON.

Sique tuum pectus contingat spesve metusve,
  Quæ tibi non dederit blandus et asper amor,
Hinc procul, erro levis! nondum urere—cuncta tyrannus
  Nam regit imperio, cum regit, iste fero.

Atqui si fueris, puer, ah! tam proditus, adsis;
  Ut, quid uterque gemat, discere uterque queat.
Quisquis enim quamcunque ita perdite amaveris, eheu!
  Invenies nullam, quæ tibi prosit, opem.

F. W.

QUOD FECERIT IOANNES HORNER.

ANGULUS in camera quam conspicis ille tenebat
Jampridem Hornerum puerili ætate sedentem;
Atque ibi signarent cum Saturnalia brumam,
Ornarentque omnes bellaria mystica mensas,
Parvus Ioannes sacratum et dulce comedit
Artocreas, simplexque legens sibi pollice prunum
Aiebat placide—'Puerorum en optimus ipse!'

F. H.

VERSIO ALTERA.

HORNER IACCULO sedit in angulo
Vorans, ceu serias ageret ferias,
  Crustum dulce et amabile:
Inquit et unum extrahens prunum—
'Horner, quam fueris nobile pueris
  'Exemplar imitabile!'

H. D.

SWEET ECHO.

Sweet Echo, sweetest nymph, that livest unseen
    Within thy aery shell,
  By slow Meander's margent green,
  And in the violet-embroidered vale,
    Where the love-lorn nightingale
Nightly to thee her sad song mourneth well:
Canst thou not tell me of a gentle pair
    That likest thy Narcissus are?
    O! if thou have
Hid them in some flowery cave,
    Tell me but where,
Sweet queen of parley, daughter of the sphere!
So may'st thou be translated to the skies,
And give resounding grace to all heaven's harmonies.
                MILTON.

MARMION TO CLARE.

O woman, in our hours of ease
Uncertain, coy, and hard to please,
And variable as the shade
By the light quivering aspen made;
When pain and anguish wring the brow,
A ministering angel thou!
                SCOTT.

DULCIS ECHO.

Nympha, quam leni refluentis amne
Ripa Mæandri tenet, ambiente
Aeris septam nebula, uvidique
  Marginis herba;
Sive te valles potius morantur
Roscidis pictæ violis, amorem
Qua suum noctu Philomela dulci
  Carmine luget;
Ecqua, Narcissi referens figuram,
Visa te fratrum species duorum
Movit? ah si qua, Dea, sub caverna
  Furta recondis,
Dic mihi qua nunc, male te secuti,
Florea tecum lateant in umbra,
Vocis argutæ domina et canori
  Filia cœli!
Sic et in sedem redeas paternam,
Et, chori dum tu strepitum noveni
Æmulans reddis, geminentur ipsis
  Gaudia Divis.

        E. H.

MARMIO AD CLARAM.

Femina, quæ, resides si quando carpimus horas,
 Mobilis, et dubia quæ placitura vice;
Fronde levi levior; tremulaque incertior umbra,
 Quam facit alternis populus alba comis:
Cum dolor atque supercilio gravis imminet angor,
 Fungeris angelico sola ministerio.

       H. J. T. D.

OFT IN THE STILLY NIGHT.

Oft in the stilly night,
  Ere slumber's chain has bound me,
Fond Memory brings the light
  Of other days around me.
The smiles, the tears, of boyhood's years,
  The words of love then spoken;
The eyes that shone, now dimmed and gone;
  The cheerful hearts now broken.

Oh oft as I remember all
  The friends thus linked together,
Whom I have seen around me fall
  Like leaves in wintry weather;
I feel like one who stands alone
  In banquet hall deserted,
Whose lights are fled, whose garlands dead,
  And all but he departed!

MOORE.

BABY BUNTING.

Bye baby bunting,
Father's gone a hunting,
Mother's gone a milking,
Sister's gone a silking,
Brother's gone to buy a skin
To wrap Baby Bunting in.

GAMMER GURTON.

AD ABSENTES AMICOS.

Sæpe mihi, dum nox late silet, ante catena
  Quam domitos sensus vinxerit alma quies,
Præteritos reparat magica dulcedine soles
  Mnemosyne, cupida sollicitata prece.
Omne redit quidquid ridere aut flere solebam,
  Quidquid et effari motus amore puer;
Qui nunc luce carent, oculi effulgere videntur;
  Quæ periere, novo corda lepore micant.

Ah quoties animo veteres reminiscor amicos,
  Indelibata pectora juncta fide,
Quos ego, væ misero, vidi cecidisse superstes,
  Ut folia hyberno flamine rapta cadunt;
Deserta videor spatiari mœstus in aula,
  Quam nuper festi perstrepuere chori;
Qua lychni sine luce manent, sine odore corollæ;
  Et, de convivis tot modo, solus ego!

B. H. K.

AD INFANTEM.

Venando pater est intentus: parve, quiesce;
  Mulgendo mater: parve, quiesce, puer.
Mercatum soror it bombycina syrmata: frater
  Vellus emit tenerum quod tua membra tegat.

F. H.

AULD LANG SYNE.

Should auld acquaintance be forgot,
    And never brought to min'?
Should auld acquaintance be forgot,
    And days o' lang syne?

For auld lang syne, my dear,
    For auld lang syne,
We'll tak a cup o' kindness yet,
    For auld lang syne.

We twa hae run about the braes,
    And pu't the gowans fine;
But we've wandered mony a weary foot
    Sin' auld lang syne.

We twa hae paidl't in the burn
    From morning sun till dine;
But seas between us braid hae roared
    Sin' auld lang syne.

And here's a hand, my trusty fier,
    And gie's a hand o' thine;
And we'll tak a right good willie waught,
    For auld lang syne.

And surely ye'll be your pint-stoup,
    And surely I'll be mine;
And we'll tak a cup o' kindness yet,
    For auld lang syne.

TEMPUS ACTUM.

Priscorum immemores esse sodalium,
Lapsis ex animo quos adamavimus,
Priscorum immemores esse sodalium et
    Acti temporis—hoc decet?

Acti, care comes, temporis ob dies,
Acti, fide. comes, temporis ob dies,
Spumantis pateram combibe Cæcubi
    Acti temporis ob dies

Flores in calathis nos amaranthinos
Una per juga quot devia legimus!
Sed lassos peregre traximus heu! pedes
    Acti temporis a die.

Quin solem ad medium margine fontium
Certatim vitreo flumine lusimus:
Atqui inter fremuit nos mare fluctuum
    Acti temporis a die.

Amplexum, comes o fide, morabimur
Dulcem—labra labris et manibus manum?
Depromptæ quis erit jam modus amphoræ
    Acti temporis ob dies!

Potantes cyathi lege videbimus
Uter Threiciam siccet amystidem:
Plenum fundite, Io, fundite Cæcubum
    Acti temporis ob dies!

For auld lang syne, my dear,
  For auld lang syne,
We'll tak a cup o' kindness yet,
  For auld lang syne.

                    BURNS.

FOUR AND TWENTY TAILORS.

FOUR and twenty tailors
  Went to kill a snail;
The best man among them
  Durst not touch its tail!
She put out her horns
  Like a little dun cow;
Run, tailors, run,
  Or she'll kill you all now!

             GAMMER GURTON.

THE KISS.

O LADIE faire,
When by that holie Boke I see thee sweare,
  Thinketh mine hearte,
Oh what an ever blessed Page thou art!
  Marrie, give me that kisse,
The drie regardlesse Prynte wotteth not what it is.

              SUCKLING.

Acti, care comes, temporis ob dies,
Acti, fide comes, temporis ob dies,
Spumantis pateram combibe Cæcubi
Acti temporis ob dies.

H. D.

SEX QUATER SARTORES.

Sex quater exibant sartores impete magno,
Viribus ut junctis limax spumosa periret:
Nec fuit e numero qui auderet tangere caudam!
Cornua nam extrudens sævissima, sicut in agris
Vacca rubens et nigra, croci contincta colore,
Illa suos hostes tremefecit—Abite fugaces
Sartores! vos dira manent dispendia vitæ,
Præsentemque viris intentant omnia mortem!

F. H.

BASIUM.

Cum labra imponens sacrum premis ore libellum,
Præstans juratam, pulcra Maria, fidem;
Quam vellem liber iste forem!—mihi basia serva;
Non capit illecebras arida charta tuas.

H. H.

BILLY TAILOR.

Billy Tailor was a brisk young fellow,
  Full of mirth and full of glee,
And his heart he did discover
  To a maiden fair and free.

Four and twenty press gang fellows,
  Dressed they was in blue array,
Laid cruel hands on Billy Tailor:
  Him they caught and sent to sea.

But his true love followed a'ter
  By the name of Robert Carr,
Her lily-white hands were daubed all over
  With the nasty pitch and tar.

And in the very first engagement,
  Manfully she fought among the rest;
Till a bullet blew her jacket open,
  And discovered her snow-white breast:

Which when the Captain saw—' What squall, pray,
  Hath blown you hither, Ma'am?'—says he.
' Sir, I seeks my Billy Tailor,
  Whom you pressed and sent to sea.'

GULIELMUS SARTOR.

Fortis in apricæ Gulielmus flore juventæ
Oris erat lepidi lætitiæque satur;
Celatamque diu flammam detexit amicæ,
Quæ pulcra atque animi liberioris erat.

Sex quater insiliunt Caci crudeliter illum,
Cœrulea Oceani veste notante gregem;
Vique coegerunt celsam conscendere navim,
Proh scelus! et rigidis imposuere foris.

Sed sua, de cunctis longe fidissima nautis,
Susanna est habitu pone secuta mari:
Candida in imberbi maculantur lilia vultu,
Et manus in nigram vertitur alba picem.

Illa, virum ritu, furit in certamine primo
Obsita sulphureis, nec tremefacta, globis,
Horrisonos ignes inter; dum, veste soluta,
Purior intacta est prodita mamma nive:

Qua visa Ductor—'Quisnam huc te ventus adegit?'
Postulat; 'Ereptum quærimus,' illa, 'procum;
Quem tu prendisti fecistique ire per altum!'—
'Hunccine amas? eheu, quam tibi læsus amor!

'If you seeks your Billy Tailor,
    Know he's inconstant and severe.'
(Poor Sukey's heart beat high and heavy,
    And she dropped one very big tear.)

'Rise up early in the morning,
    At rise of sun and break of day,
And you'll see your Billy Tailor
    Dancing with a lady gay.'

Then she called for sword and pistol,
    Which did come at her command,
And she shot young Billy Tailor
    With his lady in his hand.

Which when the Captain came for to know o' it,
    He very much applauded what she had done;
And he made her the First Lieutenant
    Of the gallant Thunderbomb.

                                    OLD BALLAD.

BONNIE LASS.

BONNIE lass, bonnie lass, will you be mine?
Thou shalt neither wash dishes nor serve the swine;
But sit on a cushion and sew up a seam,
And thou shalt have strawberries sugar and cream.

                                    GAMMER GURTON.

' Nam scito, infelix, inconstantem atque severum,
  Pro quo tot tuleris semivir, esse virum.'
(Vix se continuit Susannæ pectus anhelum,
  Lacrymaque ex oculis repperit una viam.)

' Surge age, et Auroræ primo sub lumine flavæ,
  Desere pendentem, sole oriente, torum ;
Quem sequeris, cantu et fidibus saltare videbis
  Ad Dominæ motus, candida et illa, suæ.'

Continuo sibi tela furens letalia poscit :
  Itur—et in digitis ignis et ensis erant ;
Stravit et atroci plumbique et sulphuris ictu
  Prensantem, interitus quæ sibi causa, manu.

Virtutis Dux magnanimæ non immemor illi
  Plausus, quos cuperet Penthesilea, dedit :
Nec mora ; fulmineæ præfecit Amazona puppi,
  Ut Legatorum de grege prima foret.

                                        H. D.

PULCRA PUELLA.

Pulcra puella, velis fieri mea, pulcra puella ?
Pascere non porcos tibi non detergere lances
Curæ erit ; at vestem suere et requiescere sella ;
Mellaque erunt epulis et lacte fluentia fraga.

                                        F. H.

THE PALACE OF ICE.

No forest fell
When thou would'st build; no quarry sent its stores
To enrich thy walls; but thou didst hew the floods,
And make thy marble of the glassy wave.
In such a palace Aristæus found
Cyrene, when he bore the plaintive tale
Of his lost bees to her maternal ear:
In such a palace poetry might place
The armoury of winter, where his troops,
The gloomy clouds, find weapons, arrowy sleet,
Skin-piercing volley, blossom-bruising hail,
And snow that often blinds the traveller's course,
And wraps him in an unexpected tomb.
Silently as a dream the fabric rose,
No sound of hammer or of saw was there,
Ice upon ice, the well-adjusted parts
Were soon conjoined, nor other cement asked
Than water interfused to make them one.
Lamps gracefully disposed and of all hues
Illumined every side; a watery light
Gleamed through the clear transparency, that seemed
Another moon new-risen, or meteor fallen
From heaven to earth, of lambent flame serene.

COWPER.

PALATIUM GLACIALE.

Non tibi, cum tantas auderes tollere moles,
Sylvæ cessit honos, non vivis hausta metallis
Saxa nec effossæ crevere in mœnia quadræ :
Ecce, tibi vitrei riguerunt marmore fluctus !
Qualis Aristæum Cyrenes regia matris
Cepit, apum strages infectaque mella querentem ;
Aut qualem sibi munit Hyems (ita fingere vates
Crediderim) diris ut servet in ædibus arma,
Si poscant sibi tela dari Ventique Nivesque,
Si jaculum glaciale pruiniferasque pharetras.
Surrexit tacite, ceu muta insomnia, moles ;
Non crepitus serræ, sonuit non verbere surdo
Malleus : ipsa super glacies illisa coactam
Firmavit glaciem, numerosaque fluxit in unum ;
Lympharumque domus lympharum aspergine crevit.
Lampades hinc intus multisque coloribus ignes
Fulgere ; transmissæ pallescere lucis imago :
Nempe aliam in terris credas consurgere lunam,
Delapsasque polo stellas atque uvida signa.

C. M.

JACKY'S FIDDLE.

JACKY, come give me thy fiddle,
  If ever thou mean to thrive.
Nay, I'll not give my fiddle
  To any man alive.
If I should give my fiddle,
  They'll think that I'm gone mad;
For many a joyful day
  My fiddle and I have had.

GAMMER GURTON.

TO A FRIEND.

THEE on thy mother's knees, a new born child,
We saw thee weep while all around thee smiled;
So live, that sinking to thy last long sleep,
Smiles may be thine, while all around thee weep.

SIR W. JONES.

DAMON AND JULIANA.

COUGHING in a shady grove
  Sat my Juliana;
Lozenges I gave my love
  Ipecacuanha:
From the box the imprudent maid
  Three score of them did pick;
Then sighing tenderly, she said—
  'My Damon, I am sick!'

OLD PLAY.

JOHANNULI FIDES.

Trade fides illas, mihi trade Johannule, si tu
   Nobiliore velis conditione frui.—
Haud ita : nulla fides feriet manus altera nostras,
   Quisquis erit qui me talia dona roget ;
Namque carens fidibus merito vesanus haberer,
   Quæ tot lætificos mecum habuere dies.

                  F. H.

AD SEXTIUM.

Quum natalibus, O beate Sexti,
Tuis adfuimus caterva gaudens,
Vagitu resonis strepente cunis
In risum domus omnis est soluta.
Talis vive precor, beate Sexti,
Ut circum lacrymantibus propinquis
Cum mors immineat toro cubantis,
Solus non alio fruare risu.

                  H. J. T. D.

THYRSIS ET PHYLLIS.

In nemore umbroso Phyllis mea forte sedebat,
   Cui mollem exhausit tussis anhela sinum ;
Nec mora, de loculo deprompsi pyxida lævo,
   Ipecacuaneos exhibuique trochos.
Illa quidem imprudens medicatos leniter orbes
   Absorpsit numero bisque quaterque decem ;
Tum tenero ducens suspiria pectore, dixit—
   ' Thyrsi, mihi stomachum nausea tristis habet.'

                  S. B.

THE DESERTED VILLAGE.

How often have I paused on every charm,
The sheltered cot and cultivated farm,
The never-failing brook and busy mill,
The decent church that topt the neighbouring hill,
The hawthorn bush, with seats beneath the shade,
For talking age and whispering lovers made!
How often have I blest the coming day,
When toil remitting lent its turn to play,
And all the village train from labour free
Led up their sports beneath the spreading tree;
While many a pastime circled in the shade,
The young contending as the old surveyed;
And many a gambol frolicked o'er the ground,
And slights of art and feats of strength went round;
And still as each repeated pleasure tired,
Succeeding sports the mirthful band inspired;
The dancing pair that simply sought renown
By holding out to tire each other down;
The swain mistrustless of his smutted face,
While secret laughter tittered round the place;
The bashful virgin's sidelong looks of love,
The matron's glance that would those looks reprove!
These were thy charms, sweet Village; sports like these
With sweet succession taught even toil to please;
These round thy bowers their cheerful influence shed;
These were thy charms—but all these charms are fled.

GOLDSMITH.

VILLA DESERTA.

Ah! quoties illo veneres miratus in agro
  Tranquillas vidi culta per arva casas,
Et loca qua pistrina sequacibus adstrepit undis,
  Mundaque vicinis addita templa jugis,
Et frutices lætos, aptasque sedentibus umbras,
  Seu senium musset, sive susurret amor.
Ah! quoties grato venerabar pectore lucem,
  Cum misso exciperent pensa labore joci,
Et paganorum properaret in agmine turba,
  Libera sub patula ducere fronde choros!
Tum fuit umbrosa quantum certamen arena!
  Colludunt juvenes, aspiciuntque senes;
Innumerosque cient vexato in gramine ludos,
  Membrorum vegeta vi, celerique manu.
Displiceat toties eadem repetita voluptas?
  Inveniet ludos læta caterva novos.
Certatim innocuam qui produxere choream,
  Ut pedibus simplex gloria parta foret;
Rusticus inspersa fœdus fuligine vultum,
  Qui movet occultos nescius ipse jocos;
Virginis indictam prodentia lumina flammam,
  Quæque oculo mater vix prohibere velit:
Has inter veneres, sedes dilecta, laboris
  Dulcibus immisti lene placebat onus;
Hæc circum placidam spirabant undique pacem;
  Hæc tibi—sed notos deseruere locos!

L.

HEY DIDDLE DIDDLE.

Hey diddle diddle! the cat and the fiddle!—
　The cow jumped over the moon;
The little dog laught to see such fine sport;
　And the dish ran away with the spoon.

Gammer Gurton.

WOE'S ME!

Oh! how hard it is to find
The one just suited to our mind!
　And if that one should be
False, unkind, or found too late,
What can we do but sigh at fate,
　And sing, ' Woe's me! woe's me!'?

Love's a boundless burning waste,
Where Bliss's stream we seldom taste,
　And still more seldom flee
Suspense's thorns, Suspicion's stings:
Yet somehow Love a something brings
　That's sweet, e'en when we sigh ' Woe's me!'

Campbell.

LITTLE BOPEEP.

Little Bopeep has lost her sheep,
　And does not know where to find them:
Let them alone, and they'll soon come home,
　And bring their tails behind them.

Gammer Gurton.

HEI DIDULUM.

Hᴇɪ didulum! atque iterum didulum! Felisque Fidesque!
Vacca super Lunæ cornua prosiluit:
Nescio qua catulus risit dulcedine ludi;
Abstulit et turpi Lanx cochleare fuga.

H. D.

EHEU!

Hᴇᴜ queis artibus invenire fas est
Illam ex omnibus una quæ puellis
Uni conveniat puella cordi?
Quæ si perfida sit maligniorve
Aut sera nimium reperta vita,
Quid restat, nisi fata ut increpantes
' Eheu!' carmine flebili sonemus?

Amor Marmaricas refert arenas,
Qua raris recreamur ora lymphis.
Spinas Ille alit asperi timoris,
Suspectæque malum fide venenum.
Atqui nescio quas Amor per artes
Dulce nescio quid feret, vel ' eheu!'
Ægra flebiliter sonante lingua.

A. M.

PARVA BOPÆPIA.

Pᴀʀᴠᴀ vagabundos Bopæpia perdidit agnos,
   Nescia secreti quo latuere loci;
Bellula, eant, abeant; ad pascua nota redibunt,
   Et reduces caudas post sua terga gerent.

H. D.

OH NO WE NEVER MENTION HER.

Oh no: we never mention Her!
  Her name is never heard:
My lips are now forbid to speak
  That once-familiar word.
From sport to sport they hurry me,
  To banish my regret;
And when they win a smile from me,
  They think that I forget.

They bid me seek in change of scene
  The charms, that others see;
But, were I in a foreign land,
  They'd find no change in me.
'Tis true, that I behold no more
  The valley where we met;
The hawthorn-tree no more I see—
  But how can I forget?

They tell me, she is happy now,
  The gayest of the gay;
They say, that she forgets me—but
  I heed not what they say;
Like me, perhaps she struggles with
  Each feeling of regret:
But, if she loved as I have loved,
  She never can forget.

HAYNES BAYLEY.

AH EJUS NUNQUAM MENTIO.

Aʜ ! Ejus nunquam mentio fit,
  De Illa siletur :
Nomen—tam notum olim—fari
  Haud mi conceditur.
Ad varios me lusus trahunt,
  Ne defleam sortem ;
Et sicubi subrisero,
  Credunt immemorem.

Loco mutato ut gaudeam,
  Par ceteris, monent :
At, ut peregre absim, mei
  Mutatum nil cernent.
Convallem, qua convenimus,
  Frustra quidem quæro,
Fagumque :—at obliviscier
  Ah ! quo queam modo ?

Illam felicem prædicant,
  Immo hilarissimam ;
Nostrique—at haud putavero—
  Affirmant oblitam.
Premit dolorem forsitan,
  Ut nos ; amaverit
At ut nos, obliviscier
  Ah ! nunquam poterit.

                              F. W.

THE HIGH-METTLED RACER.

SEE the course thronged with gazers : the sports are begun :
The confusion but hear! ' I'll bet you, Sir'—' done,' ' done!'
Ten thousand strange clamours resound far and near ;
Lords, hawkers, and jockies assail the tired ear !
While with neck like a rainbow, erecting his crest,
Pampered, prancing, and pleased, his nose touching his breast,
Scarcely snuffing the air, he's so proud and elate,
The high-mettled Racer starts first for the plate.

Now Reynard's turned out, and o'er hedge and ditch rush
Hounds, horses, and huntsmen, all hard at his brush ;
They run him at length, and they have him at bay,
And by scent and by view cheat a long tedious way ;
While alike born for sports of the field and the course,
Always sure to come through, a staunch and fleet horse,
When fairly run down the fox yields up his breath,
The high-mettled Racer is in at the death.

Grown aged, used up, and turned out of the stud,
Lame, spavined, and wind-galled, but yet with some blood,
While knowing postilions his pedigree trace,
Tell his dam won that sweepstakes, his sire gained this race,
And what matches he won too the ostlers count o'er,
As they loiter their time at some hedge-alehouse door ;
While the harness sore galls, and the spurs his sides goad,
The high-mettled Racer's a hack on the road.

ARION.

En Circum, en humeris densam concurrere turbam!
Audin' commissis post tintinnabula ludis
Qui strepitus sit Nobilium! quibus institor aures
Vocibus obtundantque Equites! placet omnibus audax
Sponsio.—Cervicem interea sinuavit in arcum,
Elatusque micat, vix captans naribus auras,
Et cute curatus plausus abit inter amicos,
Non dubius primo certamine victor, Arion.

Nunc sylvæ excutitur Vulpes penetralibus imis,
Quam citus insequitur caudæque insistere gestit
Venator, nec equos patitur catulosve morari.
Non illum sepes, non muri, nulla retardant
Flumina, dum prædam videt aut confidit odori,
Longum iter et durum studio fallente laborem.
Lassa ad mortiferum tandem se colligit ictum
Victima; cui pariter circo et venatibus aptus
Instat ovans, equitemque videt celer atque fidelis
Pulcrum ferre manu caudæ gestamen Arion.

Jam senior, titubans, nec ut olim habitator equilis,
Turgidus et planta, cum duxerit ilia, claudus,
(Nec patrii interea vetulo nil sanguinis hæret;)
Dum genus aurigæ indagant ab origine prima
Et veterum gnari memorant spolia ampla parentum;
Dum stans ad limen cauponæ ignavus agaso
Quos tulerit, cyathos inter crepat, ipse triumphos;
Dum ferrum costas, urunt et ephippia dorsum,
Tædia iniqua viæ perfert jejunus Arion.

Till at last having laboured, drudged early and late,
Bowed down by degrees, he bends to his fate ;
Blind, old, and feeble, he tugs round a mill,
Or draws sand, till the sand of his hour-glass stands still.
And now cold and lifeless, exposed to the view,
In the very same cart which he yesterday drew,
While a pitying crowd his sad relics surrounds,
The high-mettled Racer is sold for the hounds.

DIBDIN.

THE BATTLE OF GLADSMUIR.

The Battle of Gladsmuir, it was a noble stour,
  And weel do we ken that our young Prince won:
The gallant Lowland lads, when they saw our tartan plaids,
  Wheeled round to the right and away they run !

For Master Johnnie Cope, being destitute of hope,
  Took horse for his life and left his men ;
In their arms he put nae trust, for he kenned it wa' just,
  That the king should enjoy his ain agen.

JACOBITE SONG.

LADYBIRD.

Ladybird, ladybird, fly away home ;
Your house is on fire, your children will burn.

GAMMER GURTON.

Heu! multam ad noctem surgente a sole laborans
Paulatim extremam curarum vergit ad horam;
Cæcus enim et longa macie confectus et annis
Perpetuos ægre peragit sub verbere gyros:
Aut, sua dum Clepsydra vacet, trahit agmen aquarum;
Supremumque cadens, vitalem ubi reddidit auram,
In plaustro, quod heri duxit, projectus eodem,
Circumfusa dolet dum lugubre turba cadaver,
Venditur impastis canibus lacerandus Arion.

Ω.

IN MONTE GLADI.

Quam pulcris in monte Gladi certavimus armis!
  Non pugnam vicit Carolus ancipitem:
Campestres pueri, quum jam saga picta notassent,
  Dextrorsum attoniti corripuere fugam.

Copus enim super arva, ollis inglorius exspes
  Anteferens vitam, præpete currit equo;
Nil gladiis fisus, qui scibat jure potiri
  Regem iterum sceptris imperioque suo.

A. B. H.

SCARABÆA.

Parva rubens, Scarabæa, domum cito confuge pennis;
Ardet enim domus hæc, ardebit parvula proles.

F. H.

DEATH.

Ay, but to die, and go we know not where;
To lie in cold obstruction, and to rot:
This sensible warm motion to become
A kneaded clod; and the delighted spirit
To bathe in fiery floods, or to reside
In thrilling regions of thick-ribbed ice;
To be imprison'd in the viewless winds,
And blown with restless violence round about
The pendent world; or to be worse than worst
Of those, that lawless and uncertain thoughts
Imagine howling—'tis too horrible!
The weariest and most loathed worldly life
That age, ache, penury, and imprisonment
Can lay on nature, is a paradise
To what we fear of death.

SHAKESPEARE.

NOTHING CAN COME OF NOTHING.

THERE was an old woman called 'Nothing-at-all,'
Who rejoiced in a dwelling exceedingly small;
A man stretched his mouth to its utmost extent,
And down at one gulp house and old woman went.

GAMMER GURTON.

MEMENTO MORI.

ATTAMEN hinc ruere, et cæcis incurrere fatis,
    Mors ubi mundanam clauserit ista diem :
Hoc calidum torpere, putrescere ; sensile sensu
    Privari ; et fieri flexile corpus iners :
Divinam rutilis animam se mergere in undis,
    Ignea qua torret pestis, et atra sitis :
Aut arces inter septam mœrere nivales,
    Qua bruma astricto diriget usta gelu ;
Sive rapi ventis telluris mœnia circum,
    Vincula perpessam carceris aërii :
Agmina seu miserorum inter sine fine vagari,
    Per vacuas cœli jussa ululare vias :
Horribile est !—salvete, humani vos mala mundi
    Pessima, pauperies, vincla, senecta, labor !
Morte procul, mortisque metu, vos pignora adeste,
    Vos comites vitæ, sit modo vita, meæ.

                          W. J. L.

EX NIHILO NIL FIT

QUÆ ' Nihili-omnino' gaudebat nomine, tectis
    Læta perexiguis se recreabat Anus :
Stabat hiulca Gigas expandens ora, domumque
    Ah ! simul et miseram contumulabat Anum.

                          F. H.

CAROLINE.

I'll bid the hyacinth to blow,
  I'll teach my grotto green to be,
And sing my true love all below
  The holly bower and myrtle tree.

There all his wild-wood sweets to bring,
  The sweet south wind shall wander by,
And with the music of his wing
  Delight my rustling canopy.

Come to my close and clust'ring bower,
  Thou Spirit of a milder clime,
Fresh with the dews of fruit and flower,
  And mountain heath and moory thyme:

With all thy rural echoes come,
  Sweet comrade of the rosy Day;
Wafting the wild bee's gentle hum,
  And cuckoo's plaintive roundelay.

Where'er thy morning breath has played
  Whatever isles of Ocean fanned,
Come to my blossom-woven shade,
  Thou wandering wind of fairy land.

For sure from some enchanted isle,
  Where Heaven and Love their sabbath hold,
Where pure and happy spirits smile,
  Of beauty's fairest brightest mould;

CAROLINA.

Fragrare in pratis hyacinthina serta jubebo;
Instituam quernis antra virere comis;
Quaque tumens certat cum sacra laurea myrto,
    Qua peream flamma, motus amore, canam.

Illic delicias sylvarum et frigora carpens
    Felicem Zephyrus pervolitabit humum;
Cujus in amplexu et sub dulce sonantibus alis
    Secessus læti pensilis umbra tremet.

Ad mea saxa veni et crinitum frondibus antrum,
    Spiritus, Idaliis almior orte rosis;
Ferque simul floresque novos et roscida mella,
    Et cum monticola ture palustre thymum.

Concentu nemorum pleno campique susurris
    Adsis, O roseum concomitate diem;
Ad mea saxa veni, mœsta cum voce cuculli,
    Prodat et agrestem quod leve murmur apem.

Qua matutino spirasti cunque volatu;
    Quascunque Oceani luseris inter aquas;
Nunc mecum intexta requiescas floribus umbra,
    Immemor Elysii, mobilis Aura, tui.

Quippe ego crediderim fusos te nectare fontes,
    Et magici lucos deseruisse soli;
Puræ ubi sunt animæ, et Veneris pulcerrima proles,
    Et cum cœlicolis sabbata condit Amor.

From some green Eden of the deep,
 Where Pleasure's sigh alone is heaved,
Where tears of rapture lovers weep,
 Endeared, undoubting, undeceived ;

From some sweet Paradise afar
 Thy music wanders, distant, lost ;
Where Nature lights her leading star,
 And love is never, never crossed.

Oh ! gentle gale of Eden bowers,
 If back thy rosy feet should roam,
To revel with the cloudless Hours
 In Nature's more propitious home,

Name to thy loved Elysian groves,
 That o'er enchanted spirits twine,
A fairer form than Cherub loves,
 And let that name be CAROLINE !

CAMPBELL.

THE TRAVELLED PUSS.

' PUSSY cat, pussy cat, where have you been ?'
' I've been to London to see the Queen.'
' Pussy cat, pussy cat, what did you there ?'
' I frightened a little mouse under the chair.'

GAMMER GURTON.

Est, ubi forte trahit suspiria sola Voluptas,
 Insula cœruleo semisepulta mari ;
Qua læti nimium fletu solvuntur amantes,
 Nuptaque vult caro carior esse viro ;

Quidam est longinqua dulcis Paradisus in ora,
 Unde tuum labens exulat orbe melos ;
Qua parte accendit formosos Hesperus ignes,
 Pressaque sunt fidis oscula inulta genis.

Hospes ab Idaliis, Zephyre O suavissime, lucis,
 Si forte ad patriam sis rediturus humum,
Lascive cupiens cum resplendentibus Horis
 Ludere Naturæ prosperiore domo ;

Bis terque Elysios doceas resonare recessus,
 Antraque cœlestis religiosa chori,
Nomen inornatæ, Superum quæ vincat amores,
 Virginis—atque illo sit Carolina sono.

H. D.

FELIS PEREGRINABUNDA.

' Dic ubi terrarum, dulcissima Felis, abires ?'
' Augustæ in plateas, Reginam ut cernere possem.'
' Et quid in Augusta tibi contigit, optima Felis ?'
' Attonitum feci murem sub sede latentem.'

F. H.

TOM BOWLING.

HERE a sheer hulk lies poor Tom Bowling,
  The darling of our crew ;
No more he'll hear the tempest howling,
  For Death has broached him to.
His form was of the manliest beauty,
  His heart was kind and soft ;
Faithful below he did his duty,
  But now he's gone aloft.

Tom never from his word departed,
  His virtues were so rare ;
His friends were many and true-hearted ;
  His Poll was kind and fair :
And then he'd sing so blithe and jolly
  Full many a time and oft ;
But mirth is turned to melancholy,
  For Tom is gone aloft.

Yet may poor Tom find pleasant weather
  When He, who all commands,
Shall give, to call life's crew together,
  The word to pipe all hands !
Thus Death, who kings and tars despatches,
  In vain Tom's life has doffed ;
For though his body's under hatches,
  His soul has gone aloft.

DIBDIN.

AMYCLAS.

En! jacet ad cautes, sine fune phaselus, Amyclas,
    Deliciæ gregis ille marini :
Audiet haud iterum resonas super alta procellas,
    Carbasa Mors etenim contraxit.
Gratior huic aderat species, et mascula forma,
    Et probitas, et pectus amicum ;
Inter transtra fide insignis patiensque laborum,
    Nunc abiit trans culmina mali.

Huic stetit ingenium miris virtutibus auctum,
    Promissique tenax et veri ;
Carus ut ingenuis ubicunque sodalibus esset,
    Atque suæ Glyceræ jucundus.
Carmina sæpe etiam festiva voce canebat,
    Felicissimus inter nautas :
Sed læti in tacitum risus vertere dolorem ;
    Ille abiit trans culmina mali.

At tibi non gravior consurgat ventus, Amycla,
    Cum Dominus maris et terrarum
Ære ciens nautas omnes compellet in unum,
    Qui verrunt tumidum mare vitæ.
Sic, quæ finis adest nautis et regibus æque,
    Mors frustra abripuit tibi lucem ;
Nam subjecta foris quamvis tibi membra rigescant,
    Spiritus it trans culmina mali.

H. J. H.

SAUL.

' THOU, whose spell can raise the dead,
  Bid the prophet's form appear.'
' Samuel, raise thy buried head!
  King, behold the phantom seer.'

Earth yawned: he stood the centre of a cloud:
Light changed its hue retiring from his shroud:
Death stood all glassy in his fixed eye;
His hands were withered and his veins were dry:
His foot in bony whiteness glittered there,
Shrunken and sinewless and ghastly bare:
From lips that moved not and unbreathing frame,
Like caverned winds the hollow accents came.
Saul saw, and fell to earth, as falls the oak
At once, and blasted by the thunder stroke.

     ' Why is my sleep disquieted?
     Who is he that calls the dead?
     Is it thou, O King?—Behold
     Bloodless are these limbs and cold:
     Such are mine; and such shall be
     Thine to-morrow when with me.
     Ere the coming day is done
     Such shalt thou be, such thy son.
     Fare thee well! but for a day;
     Then we mix our mouldering clay.

SAULUS.

' Quæ potes obscœna voce excantare sepultos,
    Forma Sacerdotis, te duce, surgat humo !'
' Adsis ex Acheronte tuo mihi jusse, Samuel !
    Ecce ! Sacerdotis, Rex, tibi forma venit.'

Prodiit e tumulo cinctus caligine Vates,
    Pallet ab inferna veste repulsa dies ;
Lumina funereum testantur fixa soporem,
    Vena suo vacua est sanguine, dextra riget.
Candidus, et qualis solet esse silentibus umbris,
    Pes leviter nudo concutit osse solum :
Immoto tum verba labro, exanimique figura,
    Ceu cava de scopulis flamina, rauca sonant.
Vidit, et in medio procumbit pulvere Saulus :
    Non quercus citior fulmine tacta ruit.

' Cur vocor in lucem ? placidam quis suscitat umbram ?
    Ossibus et requiem non sinit esse meis ?
Regi igitur, Saulo trahor obvius ? Ecce, cadaver !
    Exsangues digitos et gelida ossa vide !
Hæc mea sunt ; et tu, quum lux jam postera fugit,
    Mecum deposito corpore talis eris.
Imo, ante æthereum quam sol compleverit orbem,
    Talis erit natus, talis et ipse pater.
Saule, brevi valeas ! paucis labentibus horis,
    Mistus erit noster tempus in omne cinis :

Thou, thy race, lie pale and low,
Pierced by shafts of many a bow;
And the falchion by thy side
To thy heart thy hand shall guide:
Crownless, breathless, headless, fall
Son and Sire, the house of Saul!"

BYRON.

BA! BA!

'Ba! ba! black Sheep,
Have you any wool?'—
'Yes, master, that we have,
Two bags full:
One for our master,
And one for our dame,
But none for the naughty boy
That lives in the lane.'

GAMMER GURTON.

LOUGH NEA.

On Lough Nea's bank as the fisherman strays
    When the clear cold eve's declining,
He sees the round towers of other days
    In the wave beneath him shining:

Thus will Memory often in dreams sublime
    Catch a glimpse of the days that are over;
Thus, sighing, look through the waves of Time,
    For the long-faded glories they cover.

MOORE.

Vulnera mille ferens cæsa cum prole jacebis;
  Fusa cruentato pallida forma solo:
Hostibus ante minax, domino nunc letifer ensis,
  Actus erit dextra per tua corda tua:
Omne pari cadet exitio; sceptrumque decusque;
  Et sua cum Sauli corpore tota domus.

W. G. H.

PRAVIS PUERIS QUOD ACCIDIT.

Bis salveto, ovium phalanx nigrorum!
Lanam, delicias meas, habetis?'
' O quidni duo sacculos habemus?
En, unum dominæ, alterum magistro!
Sed pravus puer est in angiportu,
Et pravis pueris nihil feremus.'

H. D.

IN LACU HIBERNICO.

Margine sæpe lacus errans piscator Iernes,
  Vesper ut in vitreis lucidus alget aquis,
Despicit inferius positas sub marmore turres,
  Queis notat antiquum forma rotunda decus.

Non aliter revocans sublimia somnia vidit
  Mnemosyne lapsos rursus adesse dies;
Tristisque in longa meditatur Temporis unda
  Pallida jam veterum magna tropæa ducum.

F. H.

THE BRIDESMAID.

THE bridal is over, the guests are all gone;
The bride's only sister sits weeping alone:
The wreath of white roses is torn from her brow,
And the heart of the Bridesmaid is desolate now!

With smiles and caresses she deck'd the fair bride,
And then led her forth with affectionate pride:
She knew that together no more they should dwell;
Yet she smiled when she kissed her, and whispered,
   ' Farewell!'

She would not embitter a festival day,
Nor send her sweet sister in sorrow away:
She hears the bells ringing; she sees her depart—
She cannot veil longer the grief of her heart.

She thinks of each pleasure, each pain, that endears
The gentle companion of happier years:
The wreath of white roses is torn from her brow,
And the heart of the Bridesmaid is desolate now!

                       HAYNES BAYLEY.

TO BED, TO BED, TO BED.

        Go to bed, Tom;
        Go to bed, Tom:
        Drunk or sober,
        Go to bed, Tom!

                 GAMMER GURTON.

PRONUBA.

Convivæ sponsalibus abiere ;
Sponsæ soror unica flet misere :
Disjecta corolla, rosa alba jacet,
Et Pronuba sola relicta dolet.

Quam blandula mane complexa torsit
Capillos ! foras quam superba duxit !
Victura deinceps, heu ! procul erat—
' Vale' at osculo ridens submurmurabat.

Fœdare nolebat gemendo diem ;
Sororem nolebat abire tristem—
Campana ah ! sonat, deamataque abit !—
Haud ultra dolorem deserta premit.

Annos reminiscitur actos una,
Et utrique communia læta, dura !
Disjecta corolla, rosa alba jacet,
Et Pronuba sola relicta dolet.

F. W.

AD CUBITUM.

Ad cubitum, Thoma ; cubitum, doctissime Thoma :
Ebrius aut siccus, cubitum te corripe, Thoma !

F. H.

SAMSON AGONISTES.

NOTHING is here for tears, nothing to wail,
Or knock the breast; no weakness, no contempt,
Dispraise or blame; nothing but well and fair,
And what may quiet us in a death so noble.
Let us go find the body, where it lies
Soaked in his enemies' blood; and from the stream
With lavers pure and cleansing herbs wash off
The clotted gore. I, with what speed the while
(Gaza is not in plight to say us nay)
Will send for all my kindred, all my friends,
To fetch him hence and solemnly attend
With silent obsequy and funeral train
Home to his father's house. There will I build him
A monument, and plant it round with shade
Of laurel ever green, and branching palm
With all his trophies hung, and acts enrolled
In copious legend or sweet lyric song.
Thither shall all the valiant youth resort,
And from his memory inflame their breast
To matchless valour and adventures high:
The virgins also shall on feastful days
Visit his tomb with flowers, only bewailing
His lot unfortunate in nuptial choice,
From whence captivity and loss of eyes.

MILTON.

SAMSON AGONISTES.

TALIA nec lacrymas moveant, neque pectoris ægrum
Cum gemitu planctum : neque turpe aut debile quicquam
Aut miserum video ; sed pulchræ gloria mortis,
Sed decus, et nostri superant solatia luctus.
Quin agimus : vos fœdum hostili cæde cadaver
Quærite, concretumque herbis purisque cruorem
Fontibus abluite.   Interea mihi cura propinquos
Conglomerare meos, (neque enim jam Gaza volentes
Impedit,) et pleno comitantes agmine amicos ;
Qui patrias illum, deflendum funus, ad aulas
Solennis referant per justa silentia pompæ.
Mox etiam lauro cingam monumenta perenni
Hac exstructa manu, patulaque tropæa sub umbra
Pendebunt platani, quæcunque a Marte triumphans
Abstulit ; inscriptasque viri longo ordine dotes,
Vel lyrici mira ponam dulcedine cantus.
Hæc celebrent olim fortis monumenta juventus,
Accendentque animos, ut tanta exempla colentes
Protinus intrepidi sanctæ fastigia famæ
Affectent virtute nova ; festisque diebus
Florea virgineæ fundent ibi serta catervæ,
Lævaque plorabunt hymenæi fata catenas
Artubus immisisse graves, oculisque tenebras.

L.

UNFORTUNATE MISS BAILEY.

A CAPTAIN bold in Halifax, who dwelt in country
　　quarters,
Deceived a maid, who hanged herself one morning in her
　　garters.
His wicked conscience smited him, he lost his stomach
　　daily,
Then took to drinking Ratafia, and thought upon Miss
　　Bailey.
　　Oh Miss Bailey, unfortunate Miss Bailey!
　　Oh was there ever such an unfortunate Miss Bailey!

One night he went to bed betimes for he had caught a
　　fever;
Says he, ' I am a handsome man, but I'm a gay
　　deceiver.'
His candle just at twelve o'clock began to burn quite
　　palely;
A ghost stept up to his bedside, and cried, ' Behold
　　Miss Bailey!'

' Avaunt, Miss Bailey!' then he cried, ' your face looks
　　white and mealy.'
' Dear Captain Smith,' the ghost replied, ' you've used
　　me ungenteelly:
The Crowner's quest goes hard with me because I've
　　acted frailly,
And Parson Big wont bury me, though I am dead
　　Miss Bailey!'
　　Oh Miss Bailey, unfortunate Miss Bailey!
　　Oh was there ever such an unfortunate Miss Bailey!

BALA INFORTUNATA.

Acer in hybernis Halifaxi ad mœnia ductor
  Virgineam falso prodidit ore fidem :
Illa periscelidis nodum trabe vinxit ab alta,
  Et morti infidos se dedit ulta Deos ;
Hunc impermissi torsit mens conscia facti,
  Nauseaque exanimis quotidiana gulæ ;
Acrior inque dies ardentia vina bibebat—
  Sed læsæ haud potuit non memor esse Balæ.
Heu nympha infelix, et iniquis nata sub astris !
  Infortunatæ ah perdita fata Balæ !

Quadam nocte ierat cubitum maturius æquo ;
  Febre calens jacuit, nec sopor illud erat :
Dumque ita—' Bellus ego, sed bellus proditor'—hora
  Ter quater insonuit ; pallida lampas erat ;
Umbra toro illapsa est, dixitque procaciter—' Hæc est
  Forma puellaris, frigida forma, Balæ !'

' In magnam Bala tota crucem !'—carissimus ille
  Clamitat—' os album, pollinis instar, habes.'
' O Veneri, Vulcane, tuæ quæ retia texti !
  Auctor tu sceleris, tu necis'—umbra refert ;
' In me Quæsitor Conjuratique severi
  Quod laqueo interii, quæ tua culpa, sedent :
Pontifice a pingui tumuli mihi justa negantur ;
  Nec tranem Stygios fas inhumata lacus.'
Væ mulier misera, et blando male credula amori !
  Infortunatæ ah perdita fata Balæ !

'Dear ghost,' says he, 'since you and I accounts must
    once for all close,
I have a one pound note within my regimental small
    clothes;
'Twill bribe the sexton for your grave.'—The ghost then
    vanished gaily,
Saying, 'Bless you, wicked Captain S! remember poor
    Miss Bailey!'

MORAL.

The ghost was thievishly inclined who cleared the
    Captain's riches,
For with his one pound note we find, she stole his
    leather breeches!
  Oh Miss Bailey, unfortunate Miss Bailey!
  Nor yet quite so unfortunate as rascally Miss Bailey!

                                        COLMAN.

MAT AND TOPAZ.

FULL oft with Mat does Topaz dine,
Eateth French meat and drinketh wine:
But Topaz his own verse rehearseth,
And Mat must praise what Topaz verseth.
Now sure as saint did e'er shrive sinner,
Full hardly earneth Mat his dinner!

                                        PRIOR.

Miles ad hæc—‘ Ventum est ut ad ultima, dulcis Imago,
  Viginti solidos hæc mea bracca tenet;
Hos cape, et exequias, omnis timor absit, habebis;
  Lætusque excipiet te sine lite Charon.’
Vix ea fatus erat, subitoque evanuit Umbra;
  Sique fides, vati, risus in ore fuit;
Dixit et egrediens—‘ Per faustos sis memor annos
  Infortunatæ, Dux scelerate, Balæ !’

FABULÆ ACCOMMODATIO.

Nec mora prodigiis !—cum solis vellet ad ortum,
  Quod fuerat moris, miles abire domo,
Sensit (nec fas est, qui fur sit, furta queratur)
  Cum solidis braccas surripuisse Balam !
Proh nympha infelix et iniquis nata sub astris !
  Infortunatæ ah perfida facta Balæ !

                                              H. D.

PROCILLUS ET ATTICUS.

Cœnat sæpe apud Atticum Procillus :
Illic vina dapesque sumtuosas
Sorbet ; versibus at suis citatis,
Poscit ‘ Euge σοφῶσque’ symbolam hospes.
Magni sane emis, O Procille, cœnam !

                                              F. W.

PROGRESS OF POESY.

THEE the voice, the dance obey,
Tempered to thy warbled lay.
O'er Idalia's velvet green
The rosy-crowned Loves are seen,
On Cytherea's day,
With antic sports and blue-eyed Pleasures,
Frisking light in frolic measures;
Now pursuing, now retreating,
Now in circling troops they meet:
To brisk notes in cadence beating
Glance their many-twinkling feet.
Slow melting strains their Queen's approach declare:
Where'er she turns the Graces homage pay:
With arms sublime that float upon the air,
In gliding state she wins her easy way:
O'er her warm cheek and rising bosom move
The bloom of young Desire and purple light of Love.

GRAY.

AD POESIN.

TE vox, te sequitur chorus,
Si quando liquidum protuleris melos.
    Et quum Diva potens Cypri
Natalem Idaliæ concelebrat diem,
    Tum vittis roseis Amor,
Exultatque levis turba Cupidinum,
    Ludis juncta decentibus:
Tum nudo viridem pulsat humum pede
    Audax Lætitiæ cohors:
Incedunt, celeres mox revocant gradus,
    Turmæve orbibus invicem
Occurrunt, hilares dum resonant modi,
    Concordesve pedes micant.
Adventum Veneris carmine languido
    Lenti significant soni;
En! quacunque jacit lumina, Gratiæ
    Reginam obsequio colunt.
Sublatis manibus Diva per æthera
    Molli tendit iter via;
Pulcher purpuream vibrat Amor facem,
    Læti et flamma Cupidinis
Matris perque genas perque sinum movet.

J. W. D.

THEIR GROVES O' SWEET MYRTLE.

Their groves o' sweet myrtle let foreign lands reckon,
  Where bright beaming summers exalt the perfume;
Far dearer to me yon lone glen o' green breckan,
  Wi' the burn stealing under the lang yellow broom.

Far dearer to me are yon humble broom bowers,
  Where the blue-bell and gowan lurk lowly unseen;
For there lightly tripping amang the wild flowers,
  A-listening the linnet, aft wanders my Jean.

Though rich is the breeze in their gay sunny valleys,
  And cold Caledonia's blast on the wave;
Their sweet-scented woodlands that skirt the proud palace,
  What are they?—The haunt of the tyrant and slave.

The slave's spicy forests and gold-bubbling fountains
  The brave Caledonian views with disdain;
He wanders as free as the winds of his mountains—
  Save love's willing fetters, the chains o' his Jean.

Burns.

BARNABY BRIGHT.

Barnaby Bright he was a sharp cur;
He would make a great noise if a mouse did but stir;
But now he's grown old and can no longer bark,
He's condemned by the parson to be hung by the clerk.

Gammer Gurton.

AD JOANNAM.

Suavia laudabunt alii myrteta coloni,
  Qua nitidis ridet solibus auctus odor:
Carior illa mihi filicum viret avia vallis,
  Celat ubi rivi flava genista fugam.

Carior illa humilis frondet mihi silva genistæ,
  Quas bellis latebras quas hyacinthus amat;
Inter enim flores illos, ubi vernat acanthis,
  Sæpe levem celerat nostra Joanna pedem.

Rideat æstivis peregrina in vallibus aura;
  Scotia ventoso frigore verrat aquas:
Silva quid est, celsas redolens quæ suspicit ædes?—
  Mœsta domus servi, mœsta ferocis heri.

Aurifluos Scotus fontes et odora vireta,
  Serviles, spectat fortis et odit, opes;
It vagus, it liber, patrio cum flamine—vinclis
  Solus Amor gratis, sola Joanna tenet.

B. H. K.

BARNABÆOCANDIDUS.

Barnabæocandidus Molossus acer erat,
Latrabat ille fortiter si mus se commoveret:
Nequit senex nunc latrare, et canicida Pontifex
Damnavit illum laqueo, et Clericus est carnifex.

H. D.

PEACE.

I HAVE found Peace in the bright earth,
　And in the sunny sky;
By the low voice of summer seas,
　And where streams murmur by.

I find it in the quiet tone
　Of voices that I love;
By the flickering of a twilight fire,
　And in a leafless grove:

I find it in the silent flow
　Of solitary thought,
In calm half-meditated dreams,
　And reasonings self taught.

But seldom have I found such Peace,
　As in the soul's deep joy
Of passing onward, free from harm,
　Through every day's employ.

If gems we seek, we only tire,
　And lift our hopes too high:
The constant flowers that line our way
　Alone can satisfy.

ALFORD.

THE GRENADIER.

WHO comes here?—A grenadier.
What d'ye want?—A pot of beer.
Where's your money?—I forgot.
Get you gone, you drunken sot!

GAMMER GURTON.

PAX.

Pax mihi est rident ubi læta rura :
Est mihi claro radiante cœlo,
Qua mare æstivum silet, et levis qua
Murmurat amnis.

Est in annosa sine fronde silva ;
Est ubi incerto focus igne lucet
Vesperi ; est inter placidam loquelam
Vocis amatæ :

Aut ubi soli tacitoque rerum
Ante gestarum facies recursat ;
Sive venturæ vigilantis inter
Somnia surgunt.

Omnium vero mihi Pax adesto
Illa, quæ dulcem decorat laborem,
Jussa fungenti vitio carentis
Munera vitæ.

Quid cupis gemmas? quid avarus et spe
Fessus insana nimis alta quæris?
Carpe contentus facili rubentes
Tramite flores.

W. J. L.

MILITI PROCERO QUOD ACCIDIT.

Quisnam est qui venit hic?—Miles procerus et audax.
Quidnam est quod poscis?—Da liquidam Cererem.
Ast ubi sunt nummi?—Sum nummi oblitus et expers.
Furcifer, ad corvos, ebrie, pote, tuos !

H. D.

THE MEETING OF THE SHIPS.

WHEN o'er the silent seas alone
For days and nights we've cheerless gone,
Oh those who've felt it, know how sweet
Some sunny morn a sail to meet!
Sparkling at once is every eye,
' Ship ahoy! ship ahoy!' our joyful cry;
And answering back the sounds we hear,
' Ship ahoy! ship ahoy! what cheer, what cheer?'
Then sails are backed, we nearer come;
Kind words are said of friends and home—
Till soon, too soon, we part with pain,
To sail o'er silent seas again.

MOORE.

MISTRESS MARY.

MISTRESS Mary,
Quite contrary,
　How does your garden grow?—
With silver bells
And cockle shells
　And hyacinths all of a row.

GAMMER GURTON.

NAVIUM OCCURSUS.

Cum soli in tacito per tempora longa profundo
    Ivimus æquorea nocte dieque via,
O bene queis licuit nota est animosa voluptas
    Mane sub æstivo cernere adesse ratem !
Scintillant oculis orientia gaudia ; voces
    Lætificæ resonant, ' Huc age, cymba, veni !'
' Huc age, cymba, veni !' lætis iteratur amicis :
    ' Anne vales ?'—aliis partibus, ' anne vales ?'
Carbasa se retrahunt, propiores ducimur ambæ ;
    Dulcia de cara dicta repente domo ;
Tum citius, citius divellimur, ut mare rursus
    Per solum et tacitum triste sequamur iter.

F. H.

DOMINA MARIA.

O mea Maria,
Tota contraria,
    Quid tibi crescit in horto ?—
Testæ et crotali
Sunt mihi flosculi,
    Cum hyacinthino serto.

H. D.

THE DRAMA OF LIFE.

ALL the world's a stage,
And all the men and women merely players;
They have their exits and their entrances,
And one man in his time plays many parts,
His acts being seven ages. At first the infant,
Mewling and puking in the nurse's arms:
And then the whining school-boy with his satchel
And shining morning face, creeping like snail
Unwillingly to school. And then the lover
Sighing like furnace, with a woful ballad
Made to his mistress' eyebrow. Then a soldier
Full of strange oaths, and bearded like the pard,
Jealous in honour, sudden and quick in quarrel,
Seeking the bubble reputation
Even in the cannon's mouth. And then the justice,
In fair round belly with good capon lined,
With eyes severe, and beard of formal cut,
Full of wise saws and modern instances;
And so he plays his part. The sixth age shifts
Into the lean and slippered pantaloon,
With spectacles on nose and pouch on side;
His youthful hose well saved, a world too wide
For his shrunk shank, and his big manly voice

FABULA VITÆ.

Quo partes agimus, terra est commune theatrum,
Scenaque factorum : instabiles eximus, inimus,
Fabulaque in septem vitæ producitur actus.
Principio in cunis vagit sine viribus infans,
Nutricisque sinu vomit et lallare recusat.
Inde puer querulus doctæ delubra Minervæ
Suspensus dextra loculos, et lucidus ora,
Incessu tardo adrepit : tum tristis amator
Fornacis ritu fervet, caræque puellæ
Molle supercilium lugubri carmine laudat.
Hinc bellator atrox, in jurgia promptus et audax,
Jurans per loca mira, feræ barbatus ad instar,
Vanum et inane decus vel in ipso limine mortis
Quærit ovans, vitamque cupit pro laude pacisci !
Proximus in scenam judex venit. Ille rotundo
Ventre capit pullam, lautæque opsonia mensæ,
Contractos torquens oculos, barbaque timendus ;
Verbaque docta loqui solet, et nova promere facta ;
Et sibi sic proprias partes agit. Inde senecta
Vaccillans curva titubat, macilentus homullus,
Laxa podagrosæ supponens tegmina plantæ ;
Cui pera ad latus est, et vitrea lumina nasum ;
Cui, bene servatus, jam major crure cothurnus.

Turning again toward childish treble, pipes
And whistles in his sound. Last scene of all,
That ends this strange eventful history,
Is second childishness and mere oblivion,
Sans teeth, sans eyes, sans taste, sans everything.

                                        SHAKESPEARE.

WHY SO PALE.

WHY so pale and wan, fond lover?
    Prythee, why so pale?
Will, when looking well can't move her,
    Looking ill prevail?
    Prythee, why so pale?

Why so dull and mute, fond lover?
    Prythee, why so mute?
Will, when speaking well can't win her,
    Saying nothing do't?
    Prythee, why so mute?

Quit, quit for shame! this will not move;
    This cannot take her:
If of herself she will not love,
    Nothing can make her—
    The Devil take her!

                                        SUCKLING.

Tum lingua infringi, vox delirare virilis,
Et fundi infantes balba de nare susurri.
Ocius inde ætas succedit septima—finis
Portenti, extremus vitai mobilis actus:
Claudicat ingenium, rediere oblivia rerum;
Gustus hebet, pereunt dentes, caligat ocellus;
Omnia deficiunt atque uno tempore desunt.

B. H. D.

CUR PALLES.

Cur tener palles amator?
    Fare, cur palles?
Quod rubenti denegatur,
    Tune pallens id feres?
        Fare, cur palles?

Cur puer taces amator?
    Fare, cur taces?
Eloquenti quod negatur,
    Idne tu tacens feres?
        Fare, cur taces?

Abstine, abstine, proh pudorem!
    Istud haud movet:
Sponte ni sentiat amorem,
    Nil eam flectet—
        Orcus occupet!

F. W.

THE CITY SHOWER.

CAREFUL observers may foretell the hour,
By sure prognostics, when to dread a shower.
While rain depends, the pensive cat gives o'er
Her frolics, and pursues her tail no more.
Returning home at night, you'll find the sink
Strike your offended sense with double stink.
If you be wise, then go not far to dine;
You'll spend in coach hire more than save in wine.
A coming shower your shooting corns presage;
Old aches will throb, your hollow tooth will rage;
Sauntering in coffee-house is Dulman seen;
He damns the climate and complains of spleen.

Meanwhile the South, rising with dabbled wings,
A sable cloud athwart the welkin flings,
That swill'd more liquor than it could contain,
And, like a drunkard, gives it up again.
Brisk Susan whips her linen from the rope,
While the first drizzling shower is borne aslope:
Such is that sprinkling, which some careless quean
Flirts on you from her mop, but not so clean;

IMBER URBANUS.

Si bene quis varii cognoverit omina cœli,
    Non temere huic subitis obfuit imber aquis.
Scilicet in terras ubi sit ruitura procella,
    Undique dant certas plurima signa notas.
Desinit assuetos venturi præscia ludos,
    Nec sequitur caudam felis, ut ante, suam :
Putrida corruptos sentina emittet odores,
    Cum propriam repetes, nocte ineunte, domum.
Si sapias, hodie sit cura domestica cœna ;
    Mensa nec alterius suadeat ire foras ;
Quippe gravis sumptus conductæ (crede) quadrigæ,
    Plus tibi constabit quam tua cœna domi.
Sæva dabunt importuni præsagia calli,
    Et novus a fractis dentibus angor erit.
Oscitat inque uncta discinctus Natta popina
    Multa piger de se, de Jove multa dolet.
Interea madidas Auster quatit humidus alas,
    Et totum nubes occupat atra polum,
Quæ nimio proluta haustu, velut ebrius olim,
    Indelibatas evomit ore dapes.
Suspensas Susanna rapit de cannabe vestes,
    Fertur ut obliqua prima procella via.
Sic tortis agitur de scopis fœtidus imber,
    Præter inexpertas te properante fores :

You fly, invoke the gods; then turning stop
To rail; she singing still whirls on her mop.
Nor yet the dust had shunned th' unequal strife,
But, aided by the wind, fought still for life.

Now in contiguous drops the flood comes down,
Threatening with deluge this devoted town:
To shops in crowds the daggled females fly,
Pretend to cheapen goods, but nothing buy.
The templar spruce, while every spout's abroach,
Stays till 'tis fair, yet seems to call a coach.
The tucked-up semstress walks with hasty strides,
While streams run down her oiled umbrella's sides.
Here various kinds by various fortunes led,
Commence acquaintance underneath a shed:
Triumphant tories and desponding whigs
Forget their feuds, and join to save their wigs.
Boxed in a chair the beau impatient sits,
While spouts run clattering o'er the roof by fits;
And ever and anon with frightful din
The leather sounds; he trembles from within.

Now from all parts the swelling kennels flow,
And bear their trophies with them as they go:
Filths of all hues and odour seem to tell
What street they sailed from, by their sight and smell.

Testaris Superos; fugis; ancillæque minaris;

 Illa canit; gravior fit quoque gyrus aquæ.

Ingruit interea cum multo pulvere nimbus,

 Et movet alternas sævus uterque vices.

Densior at cœlo cum tandem decidit imber,

 Guttaque jam guttam continuata premit,

Femina per madidos festinat plurima vicos;

 Admissas alias prompta taberna capit.

Quælibet expositas miratur Delia merces;

 Et nihil empturæ cuncta licentur anus.

Comptus inurbanum metitur Pollio cœlum,

 De conducendis ceu dubitaret equis:

Non lentis Phyale pedibus succincta laborat;

 In latus umbellæ flumina mille furunt.

Hic varie ductos, variis qui partibus adstant,

 Hospita colloquio congregat umbra pari;

Quique habet imperium regni, quique ardet habere;

 Regnorum immemores si loca sicca petant.

Parte alia juvenis lectica vectus operta,

 Dum sedet, effusas in caput horret aquas:

En! corium stridet, pluvias quod desuper arcet;

 Horrendus sonor est—intus et ille tremit.

Omnibus interea in plateis tumuere canales,

 Fertque simul prædam quæque cloaca suam;

They, as each torrent drives with rapid force,
From Smithfield to St Pulcre's shape their course;
And in huge confluence joined at Snowhill ridge,
Fall from the conduit prone to Holborn bridge.
Sweepings from butchers' stalls, dung, guts and blood,
Drowned puppies, stinking sprats, all drenched in mud,
Dead cats and turnip tops come tumbling down the flood.

SWIFT.

TO A LADY.

Too late I stayed, forgive the crime;
    Unheeded flew the hours:
How noiseless falls the foot of Time
    That only treads on flowers!

What eye with clear account remarks
    The ebbing of the glass,
When all the sands are diamond sparks,
    That dazzle as they pass?

Ah! who to sober measurement
    Time's happy swiftness brings,
When birds of Paradise have lent
    Their plumage to his wings?

W. SPENCER.

Utque ruunt luteum per vicum impulsa tropæa,
  Ipsa notant a queis partibus urbis eant.
Per Fora per totum violens fluit unda macellum;
  Immensos aperit longa Suburra sinus;
Hic varia effœti rapiuntur pignora vici,
  Ilia percussi mista cruore bovis,
Piscesque, immundique canes, felesque, fimusque,
  Stercus odoriferæ colluviesque viæ.
Sed mihi nec spatium est nec mens, ut singula narrem—
  Cuncta simul tumidis rapta feruntur aquis.

J. H.

AD LYDIAM.

DA veniam fasso; puduit, te absente, teneri—
  Oblitus horarum fui:
Quam tacito incedit Tempus pede, nil nisi molles
  Cum calce flores proterit!

Quis, sensim ut refluunt, ita grana fidelis ocellus
  In vitreo notat globo,
Si gemmis splendet simul omnis arena minutis,
  Nitore quæ fallunt suo?

Quis quod amat metitur opus celeremque volatum
  Inter serena Temporis,
Cum Paradisiacæ plumæ suffuderit alis
  Tempus colores aureos?

H. D.

QUEEN MAB.

Come follow, follow me,
You faery elves that be,
Which circle on the green,
Come follow Mab your queen:
Hand in hand let's dance around,
For this place is Faery ground.

When mortals are at rest,
And snoring in their nest,
Unheard and unespied
Through keyholes we do glide;
Over tables stools and shelves
We trip it with our Faery elves.

Upon a mushroom bed
Our table cloth we spread;
A grain of rye or wheat
Is manchet which we eat;
Pearly drops of dew we drink
In acorn cups filled to the brink.

The brains of nightingales,
With unctuous fat of snails,
Between two cockles stewed,
Is meat that's easily chewed:
Tails of worms, and marrow of mice,
Do make a dish that's wondrous nice.

MABELLA REGINA.

Eia! omnes celeri gradu sequentes,
Vos, quotquot Dryadum minutiorum
Circum gramineum perambulatis,
Reginam comitate vos Mabellam :
Conjunctis manibus, choro rotundo,
Sacrata saliamus hac in umbra.

Quum mortale genus, sopore victum,
Stertit pacifico toro recumbens,
Nos clavis cavitatem inire doctæ,
Quas non audiet aut videbit ullus ;
Per mensas, abacos, scabella, turmæ
Saltamus Dryadum minutiorum.

Boleti caput en! torale nostrum
Apte sustinuit ; levemque panem
Dat granum Cereris, levemque potum
Roris gutta, micans ut alba gemma,
In glandis cyatho satis capaci.

Quantum in luscinia latet cerebri,
Et testudinum adeps inunctiorum,
Cum binis cochleis perinde coctus,
Non est difficilis cibus molari :
Caudæ vermibus et medulla muri
Componunt epulas perelegantes.

The grasshopper gnat and fly
Serve for our minstrelsy.
Grace said, we dance awhile,
And so the time beguile :
And if the moon doth hide her head,
The glow-worm lights us home to bed.

On tops of dewy grass
So nimbly we do pass,
The young and tender stalk
Ne'er bends when we do walk :
Oft in the morning may be seen
Where we the night before have been.

PERCY'S RELIQUES.

BIBO.

WHEN Bibo thought fit from this world to retreat,
As full of champagne as an egg's full of meat,
He turned in the boat and to Charon he said—
' I will be rowed back, for I am not yet dead'.
' Trim the boat and sit quiet', stern Charon replied,
' You may have forgot you were drunk when you died.'

PRIOR.

Cicadæ culices simulque muscæ
Nobis harmoniam suam ministrant;
Atque actis ibi gratiis parumper
Saltamus, properantius fugantes
Noctem præcipitem: latente luna,
Lampyris radios dat alma nobis,
Et nos ad cubitum domum reducit.

Herbæ vertice roscido virentis
Tam molli pede præterimus omnes,
Ut caulis tener et recenter ortus
Non se deprimat, ambulante nostro
Conventu super: at, rubente cœlo
Auroræ radiis, videre possis,
Qua nos lusimus in priore nocte.

F. H.

BIBO.

Cum Bibo de terris tandem dignatus abire est,
   Spumantis Bacchi plenus, ut ova cibi;
Exsilit in cymba tristemque Charonta moratur—
   'Remum inhibe; non sum mortuus, ire nego.'
'Heus! cave, cymbam agitas'—cui portitor; 'O bone, nescis
   Multo prolutum te periisse mero?'

B.

ARETHUSA.

AND now from their fountains
In Enna's mountains
Down one vale where the morning basks,
Like friends once parted
Grown single-hearted,
They ply their watery tasks.
At sun-rise they leap
From their cradles steep
In the curve of the shelving hill;
At noontide they flow
Through the woods below,
And the meadows of Asphodel;
And at night they sleep
In the rocking deep,
Beneath the Ortygian shore;
Like spirits that lie
In the azure sky,
When they love but live no more.

SHELLEY.

THE CLOWN'S REPLY.

JOHN TROTT was desired by two witty peers
To tell them the reason, why Asses had ears:
' An't please you', quoth John, ' I'm not given to letters,
Nor dare I pretend to know more than my betters;
Howe'er from this time I shall ne'er see your graces,
As I hope to be saved, without thinking of Asses.'

GOLDSMITH.

ARETHUSA.

GRATA jacet vallis sub amœnæ montibus Ennæ,
    Pandit ad Eoum quæ sua rura jubar :
Hanc Arethusa colit ; colit amnis amator eandem ;
    Labitur undarum læta labore dies :
Dulce sodalitium—rediit mens una duobus ;
    Lis, modo quæ rupit, firmat amicitiam.
Cautibus exsiliunt montano mane cubili,
    Inde terunt varias prona fluenta vias ;
Pascua maturo quærunt viridantia Phœbo,
    Asphodelique novis roribus herba tumet.
Undosi demum delapsos in maris æstum
    Serior Ortygio contegit umbra sinu :
Tales sidereis animæ lætantur in arvis,
    Queis, licet effluxit vita, relucet amor.

W. J. L.

CATUS QUANTUMVIS RUSTICUS.

'NOVISTINE'—duo proceres dixere faceti—
    ' Auriculis cur gaudet Asellus,
Optime Trottorum?'—' Sum plane indoctior', ille ;
    ' Nec vobis plus scire decorum est :
' At mihi Asellorum, cum vos vidisse, Magistri,
    Contigerit, referetur imago'.

H. D.

THE QUEEN OF HEARTS.

THE Queen of Hearts,
She made some tarts
  All on a summer's day;
The Knave of Hearts,
He stole those tarts
  And took them quite away.
The King of Hearts,
He missed those tarts,
  And beat the knave full sore;
The Knave of Hearts
Brought back those tarts,
  And stole them never more.

CANNING.

POOR LUBIN.

ON his death-bed poor Lubin lies,
  His spouse is in despair:
With frequent sobs and mutual cries
  They both express their care.

'A different cause,' says Doctor Sly,
  'The same effect may give:
Poor Lubin fears that he may die,—
  His wife that he may live.'

PRIOR.

CORDIUM REGINA.

Cordium Regina fecit
Quam suavissimas placentas
Die diligens æstivo.
Cordium Fur ille primus,
Princeps idem primo natus,
Furabatur has placentas,
Penitusque subtrahebat.
Cordium Rex iracundus
Novit perditas placentas,
Acriterque verberavit
Furem simul filiumque.
Reddiditque Fur placentas,
Princeps idem primo natus,
Cordium Fur ille primus,
Neque rursum spoliavit.

F. H.

LUBINUS MORIENS.

Sub exitu Lubinus in toro jacet;
    Desperat uxor interim;
Suspiriisque, lacrymisque mutuis,
    Ambo dolores exprimunt.

'Diversa causa gignit effectus pares,'
    Mussat Sacerdos callidus;
'Mortis metu Lubinus anxius gemit—
    Ne vivat uxor anxia est.'

M.

ŒNONE.

O MOTHER Ida, many-fountained Ida,
Dear mother Ida, hearken ere I die.
Aloft the mountain lawn was dewy dark
And dewy dark aloft the mountain pine;
Beautiful Paris, evil-hearted Paris,
Leading a jet-black goat, white-horned, white-hooved,
Came up from reedy Simois all alone.

O mother Ida, hearken ere I die.
I sate alone: the golden-sandalled morn
Rose-hued the scornful hills: I sate alone
With down-dropt eyes: white-breasted like a star
Fronting the dawn he came: a leopard skin
From his white shoulder drooped: his sunny hair
Clustered about his temples like a god's:
And his cheek brightened, as the foam-bow brightens
When the wind blows the foam: and I called out—
' Welcome Apollo, welcome home Apollo,
Apollo, my Apollo, loved Apollo'.

Dear mother Ida, hearken ere I die.
He, mildy smiling, in his milk-white palm
Close-held a golden apple, lightning bright
With changeful flashes, dropt with dew of heaven
Ambrosially smelling. From his lip,
Curved crimson, the full-flowing river of speech
Came down upon my heart.

ŒNONE.

Me miseram exaudi scatebroso e culmine mater!
Ida, meam, genitrix, mors advenit, accipe vocem.
Desuper Eoo montanus rore madebat
Tractus, et in dubio stillabant lumine pinus,
Cum Paris, heu! nimium pulchri sub tegmine vultus
Turpia corda fovens, albis et cornibus hircum
Insignem et pedibus deducens, cætera nigrum,
Solus arundinea venit Simoëntis ab unda.

Ida, meam, genitrix, mors advenit, accipe vocem.
Aurea per montes roseo fulgore superbos
Ridebat veniens Aurora; ego sola sedebam
Triste tuens; illum mox albo pectore, ut astrum
Dissipat obscuras adversa fronte tenebras,
Vidi incandentem.   Lateris gestamina pulchri
Exuviæ pardi pendebant, diaque flavis
Fluctibus undantes velabant tempora crines;
Fulgebantque genæ, qualis, cum ventus aquosam
Fert agitans spumam, nitet arcus in ætheris auras.
Tunc ego: 'Mi tandem salve mihi, dulcis Apollo,
Exoptate diu salve mihi, dulcis Apollo!'

Ida, meam, genitrix, mors advenit, accipe vocem.
Ille mihi flavum, quem lactea dextra tenebat,
Splendore insolito, divini fulguris instar,
Purique ambrosios exspirans roris odores,
Porrexit malum, suavique arrisit amore.

'My own Œnone
Beautiful-browed Œnone, mine own soul,
Behold this fruit, whose gleaming rind engraven
"For the most fair", in aftertimes may breed
Deep evil-willedness of heaven and sere
Heart-burning toward hallowed Ilion;
And all the colour of my after-life
Will be the shadow of to-day.   To-day
Here and Pallas and the floating grace
Of laughter-loving Aphrodite meet
In many-folded Ida to receive
This meed of beauty, she to whom my hand
Award the palm.   Within the green hill-side,
Under yon whispering tuft of oldest pine,
Is an in-going grotto, strawn with spar
And ivymatted at the mouth, wherein
Thou unbeholden mayst behold, unheard
Hear all, and see thy Paris judge of gods.'

TENNYSON.

HUMPTY DUMPTY.

HUMPTY DUMPTY sat on a wall;
Humpty Dumpty had a great fall:
Not all the King's horses, nor all the Queen's men,
Could put Humpty Dumpty on the wall again.

GAMMER GURTON.

Protinus e roseo manantia verba labello
Cor pepulere meum—' Speciosam candida frontem,
Œnone, mea vita, hujusne in cortice mali
Inscriptum, " Capiat quæ sit pulcherrima," cernis?
Hoc gravis a pomo surget cœlestibus ira,
Invidaque incumbent sacratæ numina Trojæ;
Et mihi venturos animi vitæque colores
Hæc dabit una dies. Hodie cum Pallade et Hera
Adveniet, liquidæ mira dulcedine formæ,
Et lepido risu Cytherea, ubi devia surgit
Ida, venustatis magna ad certamina nostra
Decernenda manu. Viridem tu monte sub ipso
Speluncam insideas, ubi desuper alta susurrant
Pineta, et varios spargit Natura lapillos
Prætenditque hederas; ibi mox celata videbis
Me Paridem magnas Divarum solvere lites.'

L.

HUMTIUS DUMTIUS.

Humtius in muro requievit Dumtius alto;
  Humtius e muro Dumtius heu cecidit!
Sed non Regis equi, Reginæ exercitus omnis,
  Humti, te, Dumti, restituere loco!

H. D.

POOR ROBIN.

THE north-wind doth blow,
And we shall have snow,
And what will poor Robin do then,
                    Poor thing?

He'll sit in a barn,
And keep himself warm,
And hide his head under his wing,
                    Poor thing.

                    GAMMER GURTON.

THE TOYS OF LIFE.

BEHOLD the child, by nature's kindly law,
Pleased with a rattle, tickled with a straw.
A livelier play-thing gives his youth delight,
A little louder, but as empty quite.
Gold, garters, scarfs, amuse his riper stage,
And beads and prayer books are the toys of age;
Pleased with this bauble still, as that before;
Till tired he sleeps, and life's dull play is o'er.

                    POPE.

PAT A CAKE.

PAT a cake, pat a cake, baker's man—
So I do, master, as fast as I can.
Pat it and prick it and mark it with C,
Then it will serve for Charley and me.

                    GAMMER GURTON.

RUBECULA.

INGRUIT sævus Boreas, nivesque
Jam per algentem glomerantur auram;
Tempore hoc tristi tibi cara quid, Ru-
    becula, fiet?

Horreo tu stramineo sedebis,
Et vel hiberna glacie calescens
Dulce sub penna caput usque tu, Ru-
    becula, condes.

       F. H.

NOSTRUM ILLUD VIVERE.

ECCE modo infantem—sic Dii voluere benigni—
 Gaudeat ut crotalo, stramine captus hiet!
Acrior oblectat juvenilia pectora ludus,
 Aucto, sed pariter futilis ille, sono;
Aurumque et procerum phaleras maturior ætas,
 Votivas sequitur balba senecta nuces:
Idem amor his nugis, idemque recurrit in illis:
 Dum dormit ludo fessus, et—exit homo.

       H. D.

PISTORIS PUER.

PISTORIS puer, O dulcem mihi tunde farinam.
 Imo etiam rapida res erit acta manu.
Punge decenter acu, tituloque inscribe magistri;
 Sic mihi, sic Carolo serviet illa meo.

       F. H.

DANAE.

Ὅτε λάρνακι ἐν δαιδαλέᾳ ἄνεμος
βρέμῃ πνέων, κινηθεῖσά τε λίμνα
δείματι ἤριπεν οὐδ᾽ ἀδιάνταισι
παρείαις, ἀμφί τε Περσεῖ βάλε
φιλὰν χέρα, εἶπέν τε· ὦ τέκος
οἷον ἔχω πόνον· σὺ δ᾽ ἀώτεις γαλαθήνῳ τ᾽
ἤτορι κνώσσεις ἐν ἀτερπεῖ δώματι
χαλκεογόμφῳ δὲ, νυκτιλαμπεῖ
κυανέῳ τε δνόφῳ. τὺ δ᾽ αὐαλέαν
ὕπερθε τεὰν κόμαν βαθεῖαν
παρίοντος κύματος οὐκ ἀλέγεις,
οὐδ᾽ ἀνέμων φθόγγων, πορφυρέᾳ
κείμενος ἐν χλανίδι, πρόσωπον καλόν.
εἰ δέ τοι δεινὸν τόγε δεινὸν ἦν,
καί κεν ἐμῶν ῥημάτων λεπτὸν
ὑπεῖχες οὖας, κέλομαι, εὖδε βρέφος,
εὐδέτω δὲ πόντος, εὐδέτω ἄμετρον κακόν.
μεταβουλία δέ τις φανείη,
Ζεῦ πάτερ, ἐκ σέο· ὅτι δὴ θαρσαλέον
ἔπος, εὔχομαι τεκνόφι δίκας σύγγνωθί μοι.

SIMONIDES.

DANAE.

QUANDO insonaret sub trabe dædala
Vis sæva ventorum, et pelagi palus
   Concussa suaderet timorem,
      Inque oculis premeretur humor,

Fovit tenellum Persea brachiis
Dixitque Mater: 'Me miseram, quibus
   Curis laboro! tu sed æneis
      Vectibus implacidoque lecto,

Mollissima ætas, sterneris, et gravem
Carpis soporem: te pelagi premit
   Cœlique caligo; sed ipse
      Immemori frueris quiete;

Quantum capillis immineant aquæ,
Quantumque venti vis crepet, unice
   Securus: ut pulcher nitensque
      Purpureo recubas in ostro!

Quod si timeres quæ mihi sunt metu,
Et lene consilium imbiberes meum,
   Dormi, juberem; dormiunto
      Dura fugæ mala, dura ponti.

Sic et benignus consilium pater
Mutet refingens in melius, neque
   Hæc nolit ulcisci, precando
      Ni fuerim nimium molesta!'

                      C. M.

EUPHELIA AND CHLOE.

THE merchant, to secure his treasure,
　　Conveys it in a borrowed name:
Euphelia serves to grace my measure;
　　But Chloe is my real flame.

My softest verse, my darling lyre,
　　Upon Euphelia's toilet lay;
When Chloe noted her desire,
　　That I should sing, that I should play.

My lyre I tune, my voice I raise,
　　But with my numbers mix my sighs;
And whilst I sing Euphelia's praise,
　　I fix my soul on Chloe's eyes.

Fair Chloe blushed—Euphelia frowned:
　　I sung and gazed: I played and trembled:
And Venus to the loves around
　　Remarked, how ill we all dissembled.

PRIOR.

ROCK-A-BYE BABY.

ROCK-A-BYE Baby, upon the tree-top;
When the wind blows the cradle will rock;
When the bough breaks the cradle will fall;
Down will come cradle, baby, and all.

GAMMER GURTON.

LAVINIA ET CHLOE.

Trans mare mercator falso sub nomine currit,
  Ut vehat intactas dissimulator opes;
Non male perjuram decorat Lavinia musam;
  At mihi lux vera est, veraque flamma, Chloe.

Molle meum in thalamo cultæ Lavinia mensæ
  Addiderat carmen dulcisonamque lyram;
Quum me blanda Chloe, quod erat, cantare rogavit,
  Et non indocta verrere fila manu.

Solicito chordas, vocemque e pectore mitto;
  Sed gemitus inter carmina triste sonant:
Dumque audit falsam de se Lavinia laudem,
  Totus adorato figor in ore Chloes.

Erubuit formosa Chloe; Lavinia frontem
  Contraxit; cecini contremuique simul:
Et Venus ipsa suo ridens clamavit Amori,—
  En tria facundis prodita corda genis!

J. M.

CUNÆ ARBOREÆ.

Molliter hac, summa puer arbore, mollitur illac,
Fluctuet—hac illac: agitat cunabula ventus:
Rupta sed excutient tremulas ramalia cunas,
Omniaque illa solo, cunæ volventur et infans.

F. H.

THE ISLES OF GREECE.

The isles of Greece, the isles of Greece,
   Where burning Sappho loved and sung,
Where grew the arts of war and peace,
   Where Delos rose and Phœbus sprung!
Eternal summer gilds them yet,
But all, except their sun, is set.

The mountains look on Marathon,
   And Marathon looks on the sea;
And musing there an hour alone,
   I dreamed that Greece might still be free:
For standing on the Persian's grave,
I could not deem myself a slave.

A king sate on the rocky brow
   Which looks o'er sea-born Salamis;
And ships by thousands lay below,
   And men in nations—all were his!
He counted them at break of day—
And when the sun set—where were they?

                                   BYRON.

THE RESTLESS OLD LADY.

There was an old woman, and what do you think?
She lived upon nothing but victuals and drink;
And though victuals and drink were the chief of her diet,
Yet this restless old lady could never keep quiet.

                          GAMMER GURTON.

INSULÆ IN ÆGEO.

PLURIMA in Ægeo nitet insula plurima ponto,
    Qua Sapphus carmen quaque furebat amor ;
Unde artes pacis natæ et fera munia belli,
    Surgebat Delos, Phœbus et ortus erat.
Ardet adhuc flammis arsura perennibus æstas ;
    Sed superest patrii nil nisi solis honor.

Despiciunt alti montes Marathona patentem,
    Et Marathon ponti despicit altus aquas ;
Atque ibi dum tacita mecum meditarer in hora,
    Græcia erat somnis libera facta meis.
Quippe ego, qui Persas premerem sub calce sepultos,
    Servilis poteram conscius esse jugi ?

Rex quidam, ut perhibent, saxosa in rupe sedebat,
    Oceani Salamis filia subter erat ;
Innumeræ naves super æquora lata natabant,
    Innumeræ gentes—omnia Regis opes.
Sole recensebat primo navesque virosque—
    O ubi sunt illi, sole cadente, viri ?

                            B. H. D.

ANUS ANXIA.

OLIM erat anxia anus, valde anxia—quid tibi visum est
Potando tantum, tantum se pavit edendo !
Et quanquam potu vivebat plurima et esu,
Ipsa erat æternum fulmen, lis, jurgia, clamor !

                            F. H.

GREEN GROW THE RUSHES O.

THERE's nought but care on every han'
   In every hour that passes O:
What signifies the life of man,
   If 'twere na for the lasses O?

      Green grow the rushes O:
      Green grow the rushes O:
      The sweetest hours that e'er I spent,
      Were spent among the lasses O.

The warly race may riches chase,
   An' riches still may fly them O;
An' though at last they catch them fast,
   Their hearts can ne'er enjoy them O.

      Green grow the rushes O:
      Green grow the rushes O:
      The sweetest hours that e'er I spent,
      Were spent among the lasses O.

But gie me a canny hour at e'en,
   My arms about my dearie O;
An' warly cares, an' warly men,
   May a' gae tapsalteerie O.

      Green grow the rushes O:
      Green grow the rushes O:
      The sweetest hours that e'er I spent,
      Were spent among the lasses O.

VIRENT JUNCI.

PARTE de cuncta premit atra Cura,
Omnibus quæ prætereunt in horis;
Vita quid fallax hominum valeret,
Vox puellarum nisi subveniret?

Virent junci fluviales,
  Junci prope lymphas:
Ah quam ridet, quæ me videt
  Hora inter nymphas!

Qui velint, aurum cupiant petantque;
Adsit aut aurum fugiat petentes.
Quid preces vanas licet assequantur,
Corde si nunquam placido fruantur?

Virent junci fluviales,
  Junci prope lymphas:
Ah quam ridet, quæ me videt
  Hora inter nymphas!

Vespere in molli juvat assidentem
Me meæ amplexum dare colla circum:
At viri cum divitiis rapaces,
Et simul curæ pereant edaces!

Virent junci fluviales,
  Junci prope lymphas:
Ah quam ridet, quæ me videt
  Hora inter nymphas!

Gin you're sae douce ye sneer at this,
   You're nought but senseless asses O :
The wisest man the warl e'er saw,
   He dearly loved the lasses O.

     Green grow the rushes O :
     Green grow the rushes O :
     The sweetest hours that e'er I spent,
     Were spent among the lasses O.

Auld Nature swears the lovely dears
   Her noblest work she classes O ;
Her 'prentice han' she tried on man,
   And then she made the lasses O.

     Green grow the rushes O :
     Green grow the rushes O :
     The sweetest hours that e'er I spent,
     Were spent among the lasses O !

                    BURNS.

DICK'S NOSE.

DICK cannot wipe his nostrils when he pleases,
   His nose so long is, and his arm so short :
And never cries ' God bless me !' when he sneezes,
   He cannot hear so distant a report.

              GREEK ANTHOLOGY.

Tollitis frontes mihi qui severas,
Jure vos stultum pecus audietis :
Summus in toto Sophus orbe bella
Arsit haud una tener in puella.

Virent junci fluviales,
Junci prope lymphas :
Ah quam ridet, quæ me videt
Hora inter nymphas!

Virgine exacta sibi gratulata est
Artifex Natura, operique plaudit;
Quæ rudis Martem manus expedivit,
Doctior quanto Venerem expolivit!

Virent junci fluviales,
Junci prope lymphas :
Ah quam ridet, quæ me videt
Hora inter nymphas!

J. H. M.

DE NASO RICARDI.

Ricardus nescit madidas emungere nares,
Tam longo est naso, tam brevis a cubito :
Nec si sternutat, 'fausto siet omine!' clamat ;
Tam longe amotos non capit aure sonos.

H. D.

THE MAD DOG.

Good people all of every sort
  Give ear unto my song ;
And if you find it wondrous short,
  It cannot hold you long.

In Islington there lived a man
  Of whom the world might say,
That still a godly race he ran,
  Whene'er he went to pray.

A kind and gentle heart he had
  To comfort friends and foes ;
The naked every day he clad,
  When he put on his clothes.

And in that town a dog was found,
  As many dogs there be,
Both mongrel, puppy, whelp, and hound,
  And curs of low degree.

The dog and man at first were friends ;
  But when a pique began,
The dog to gain his private ends
  Went mad, and bit the man.

CANIS RABIDUS.

AUDITE, O cives, quovis ex ordine nati,
    Et patula nostros imbibite aure modos ;
Et si forte quibus videatur perbrevis esse,
    Non faciet longam fabula tota moram.

Rure suburbano quidam vivebat, ut aiunt,
    Quo laudis nunquam dignior alter erat ;
Non parcus Superum cultor, si credimus ori,
    Ante Deos quoties flecteret ille genu.

Hostibus hic mansuetus erat, dilectus amicis,
    In cunctos miræ sedulitatis homo :
Inque dies spisso nudum velabat amictu,
    Cum sese in vestes induit ipse suas.

Illa forte canis sese stabulabat in urbe ;
    Nec mirum est—multos urbs habet illa canes.
Illic Spartanumque genus fortesque Molossi,
    Et catuli infames, squallida turba, ruunt.

Cum nondum lites indixerat unus et alter,
    Junctus amicitia cum cane vixit homo.
Inde canis, quædam, credo, sibi commoda quærens,
    Fit subito rabidus, dilaniatque virum.

Around from all the neighbouring streets
  The wondering neighbours ran,
And swore the dog had lost his wits,
  To bite so good a man.

The wound it seemed both sore and sad
  To every Christian eye;
And while they swore the dog was mad,
  They swore the man would die.

But soon a wonder came to light,
  That shewed the rogues they lied;
The man recovered of the bite;
  The dog it was that died.

                          GOLDSMITH.

THE TROPIC SUN.

AND now, my race of terror run,
Mine be the eve of tropic sun;
No pale gradations quench his ray,
No twilight dews his wrath allay;
With disk like battle-target red,
He rushes to his burning bed;
Dyes the wide wave with bloody light;
Then sinks at once—and all is night.

                          SCOTT.

Undique per plateas vicinia tota cucurrit,
  Viditque horrendum constupuitque nefas ;
Delirare canem jurant, qui dente profano
  Tam sanctum haud metuit dilacerare senem.

Si qua fides oculis avidæ sapientibus urbis,
  Vulnera soliciti plena doloris erant ;
Delirare canem dum jurat quisque vicissim,
  Uno est consensu mors obeunda viro.

Sed nova decurrens prodit miracula tempus,
  Et vulgo infidos arguit esse dolos ;
Incolumis noster superest, mirantur et omnes
  Unum ex ambobus deperiisse canem.

H. J. H.

SOL ÆQUINOCTIALIS.

Confecto ecce ! mei furore cursus,
Mergar, sol velut æquinoctialis ;
Cui nec pallidulum jubar gradatim
Restinctum abluitur, nec acris ira
Sub rorante crepusculo silescit :
Orbe ardens, clypei rubentis instar,
Præceps insilit igneum cubile ;
Latas sanguinea face urit undas,
Conditur—subitoque tota nox est.

B. H. D.

EACH BOWER.

Each bower has beauty for me,
  There's a charm in each blossom that blows;
And, if absent the Lily should be,
  I shall do very well with the Rose:
If Roses are not in the way,
  I'll fly to a Hyacinth soon;
And I never will quarrel with May,
  For wanting the Roses of June.
No! no! 'tis my pleasure to chase
  Each pretty bud under the sun:
Why should I insult the whole race,
  By a silly selection of one?

I love each exotic, that deigns
  In a climate like this to expand;
And my heart its affection retains
  For the bloom of my dear native land:
In summer's gay mansions I dwell,
  And since summer so soon will be past,
Though I love her first bud very well,
  I have love in reserve for her last.
Yes! yes! 'tis my pleasure to chase
  Each pretty bud under the sun:
Why should I offend the whole race
  By a silly selection of one?

                              Haynes Bayley.

HORTUS QUISQUE.

Hortus mihi quisque placet,
　　Est flosculus quisque suavis;
Et Lilio absente, lubet
　　Memet recreare Rosis:
Extemplo Hyacinthum sequor,
　　Vaganti si Rosa desit;
Nec Maio de mense queror,
　　Quod Juniam haud genuit.
Ah! non; mihi est volupe
　　Omnem ligurire florem:
Unum seligens stolide,
　　Totum genus cur irritem?

Flos quisque mi ridet, oris
　　Qui hospes in his vigeat;
Nec floribus in patriis
　　Est, qui mihi non rideat:
Domum mihi grata præbet
　　Æstas—celeris sed abit!—
Et gemmula prima placet,
　　Nec ultima non placuit.
Sic est—mihi est volupe
　　Omnem ligurire florem:
Unum seligens stolide,
　　Totum genus cur cruciem?

F. W.

THE WISE MEN OF GOTHAM.

THREE wise men of Gotham
Went to sea in a bowl;
And if the bowl had been stronger,
My song had been longer.

GAMMER GURTON.

MIRA.

WHEN first the Siren Beauty's face
My wandering eye surveyed,
Unmoved I saw each fraudful grace,
That round th' enchantress played:

And still, with careless mien elate,
Defied the Paphian's wile;
As ambushed in a look he sate,
Or couched beneath a smile.

And still to rove I madly vowed
Along the dangerous way,
Secure, where other boasters bowed
Before the tyrant's sway.

Nor learned my breast to heave the sigh,
Or pour the secret heart;
Till Mira from her beamy eye
Despatched th' unerring dart.

TRES PHILOSOPHI GOTAMIENSES.

Tres Gotami quondam sapientes spiritus audax
Impulit Oceanum parvo transcurrere labro ;
Fortius hoc fuerat si vas, magis utile ponto,
Tu plura audires, ego carmina plura dedissem.

F. H.

MIRA.

Lumina cum primum, memini, juvenilia cepit
  Virgineo quicquid ludit in ore decus,
Tutus ab illecebris veneres mirabar inermes :
  A nobis famam nulla puella tulit.

Hinc animo audaci nimium vultuque superbo
  Spernebam Paphii mollia tela Dei ;
Seu roseo insidias struxit male fidus in ore,
  Seu risus inter retia texit Amor.

Sæpe quidem dixi, fallacis nescius auræ,
  Me tuto angustam posse tenere viam ;
Imprudens nimium ! qui me tam sæpe negavi,
  Cætera qui vincit, vincere posse Deum.

Nam neque adhuc noram tristi suspiria cura
  Ducere, nec querulæ tangere fila lyræ ;
Cum Mira ex oculis, Phœbei fulguris instar,
  Misit vindictæ tela ministra suæ.

' Fly, fatal shaft,' with cruel zeal
  The conscious murtheress cried,
' And teach yon haughty boy to feel
  The anguish due to pride.'

To soothe the soul-subduing power
  Awhile I fondly strove ;
But combated, alas ! in vain,
  The omnipotence of Love.

Then ah ! at length, stern Power, forbear,
  Thy wrath at length forego :
Enough my youth has felt of care ;
  Enough has tasted woe.

Or if ordained by stubborn fate
  To drag the eternal chain,
Doomed, as I bend beneath its weight,
  To court relief in vain ;

To Mira equal toil impart ;
  On her thy pang bestow ;
Thrill with Love's agony her heart,
  And bid her suffer too.

                              WRANGHAM.

' I, fuge,' fatalis clamavit conscia plagæ,
  ' I, pete,' ait, ' durum, fida sagitta, latus :
Hinc tandem, hinc discat nostri contemptor oportet,
  Quæ sint feminea vulnera missa manu.'

Pectoris ut sævos possem sanare dolores,
  Tentavi medica quicquid in arte fuit ;
Sed frustra petii duro me opponere morbo :
  Ah ! medica non est arte fugandus Amor.

Improbe, parce, Puer, pennatum intendere ferrum ;
  In me crudeles desine ferre minas :
Præteritos egi non tam feliciter annos ;
  Experta est varias nostra juventa vices.

Sin quæ dispensant mortalia fila sorores
  Imposito prohibent solvere colla jugo ;
Si me fata jubent æternam ferre catenam,
  Nec prodest votis solicitasse Deos ;

Tu saltem Miræ similem, Puer, incute plagam,
  Languescat, quæso, vulnere nympha pari :
Hæc quoque cognoscat quid sit succumbere amori,
  Transadigatque animas una sagitta duas.

                                        G. C.

LOUISA.

Though by a sickly taste betrayed
Some may dispraise the lovely maid,
   With fearless pride I say,
That she is healthful, fleet and strong,
And down the rocks can leap along
   Like rivulets in May.

And smiles has she to earth unknown ;
Smiles, that with motion of their own
   Do spread and sink and rise ;
That come and go with endless play,
And ever as they pass away
   Are hidden in her eyes.

She loves her fire, her cottage-home,
Yet o'er the moorland will she roam
   In weather rough and bleak ;
And when against the wind she strains,
O might I kiss the mountain rains
   That sparkle on her cheek.

LOUISA.

Rusticam spernant alii puellam, et
Simplici myrto folia allaborent;
Suscipit gratum mea lingua munus
   Ausa referre,

Quam salus illam decoret vigorque;
Quamque veloci pede per profunda
Saxa decurrat, redeunte sicut
   Flumina Maio.

Ridet huic risus similis Dearum,
Qui suas toto veneres in ore
Prodit, alterno refluens fluensque
   Molliter æstu;

Pertinax circumvolitare lusu
Sedulo frontem; aut roseum cubile
Deserens vultus, oculi in protervis
   Ignibus abdi.

Parvulo contenta focum paternum
Et lares parvos amat: at procellæ
Immemor grata vice pervagatur
   Devia montis;

Dumque ibi in ventos animosa certat,
Imbrium gemmas utinam oscularer,
Qui genis in purpureis pudica
   Luce coruscant!

Take all that's mine beneath the moon,
If I with her but half a noon
   May sit beneath the walls
Of some old cave or mossy nook,
Whene'er she wanders up the brook
   To hunt the waterfalls.

WORDSWORTH.

THE KNIGHT'S GRAVE.

WHERE is the grave of Sir Arthur O'Kellyn
   Where may the grave of that good man be?
By the side of a fount on the breast of Helvellyn,
   Under the twigs of a young birch tree.
The oak that in summer was pleasant to hear,
And rustled its leaves at the fall of the year,
And bellowed and whistled in winter alone,
Is gone—in its place the birch tree is grown.
      The knight's bones are dust,
      And his good sword rust—
      His soul is with the saints I trust!

COLERIDGE.

Deme quot rerum videt alta Luna,
Sit reclinato mihi cum puella
Sole fervente aut veteris sub antri

    Rupe morari ;
Aut in umbroso nemorum recessu,
Fertur ut montis per amata rura, aut
Abditos fontes petit in ruentis

    Margine rivi.

          H. J. H.

ARTURI SEPULCRUM.

O ubi nunc recubant Arturi nobilis ossa?
O quibus in cippis, aut qua jacet integer herba
Ille sepulcrali?—muscoso in margine fontis
Sopitur placide gremioque Helvellynis alto :
Et super impubis betullæ virga coruscat.
Quercus enim, æstivo quæ tempore suave sonare,
Auctumnoque gravi foliis crepitare solebat,
Solaque sub brumem rauca mugire querela,
Occidit, et vacuo betulla innascitur arvo.
Pulvere cara viri commiscuit ossa vetustas,
Et fidum scabies ensem damnosa peredit—
Ordinibus spero sanctorum inscribier ipsum !

          A. B. H.

RIDE A COCK HORSE.

RIDE a cock-horse
To Banbury Cross,
To see an old woman upon a black horse:
With rings on her fingers
And bells on her toes,
She shall have music wherever she goes.

GAMMER GURTON.

HINX MINX.

HINX, Minx! the old witch winks
The fat begins to fry:
There's nobody at home but jumping Joan,
And father, mother, and I!

GAMMER GURTON.

I PUER.

I, PUER, acer eques : rapiat te mobile lignum,
Crux ubi Banburiæ plateas exornat avitas,
Ut vetulam nigro videas equitare caballo :
Cui gemmæ in manibus, cui tintinnabula plantis
Plurima, concordi sonitu comitantur euntem.

F. H.

ALTERA VERSIO.

INFANS, quadrivium ad Banburiensium
Manno te celerem corripe ligneo :
Nigro vectam ibi equo conspicies anum.
En quinque in digitis sex habet annulos,
Tintinnabula sex in digitis pedum !
Felix, dulce melos, quod ciet undique,
    Quoquo vertitur audiet.

B.

HINC HECATE.

'HINC et abhinc, Hecate !'—mala anus præ limine nictat ;
    Sibilat inferni conscius ignis adeps—
'Sola domi invenies salientia crura Joannæ'—
    Meque ipsam et matrem cum genitore meam.

H. D.

TO MISTER LAWRENCE.

LAWRENCE, of virtuous fathers virtuous son,
Now that the ways are dank, and fields all mire,
Where shall we sometimes meet and by the fire
Help waste a sullen day, what may be won
From the hard season gaining? Time will run
On smoother till Favonius re-inspire
The frozen earth, and clothe in fresh attire
The lily and rose that neither sowed nor spun.
What next repast shall feast us, light and choice,
    Of Attic taste with wine, whence we may rise
To hear the lute well touched, or artful voice
Warble immortal notes of Tuscan air.
He, who of these delight can judge and spare
    To interpose them of, is not unwise.

MILTON.

AD LAURENTIUM.

O CASTA casti progenies patris,
Dun bruma campos occupat et vias,
 Quo rure, Laurenti, reducto,
  Quosve focos apud hospitales
Longo auferemus tœdia de die?
Quod hora nobis cunque dabit lucri
 Morosa carpentes, ut annus
  Prætereat leviore penna;
Constricta donec prata refecerint
Alæ Favoni, liliaque et rosas,
 Laboris expertes, amictu
  Verna novo decorarit aura.
Quæ munda nobis cæna parabitur?
Quæ lecta mensæ fercula?—age, Attico
 De more promenturque vina, et
  Post calices bene tacta noctem
Producet una barbitos auream,
Et vox Etruscos callidior modos
 Spirare, et effundens choreæ
  Sidereæ propiora chordis.
Qui tanta novit gaudia carpere,
Prudensque parca mente frui sapit,
 Scit ille, ni fallor, Deorum
  Muneribus sapienter uti.

       H. J. K.

THE LAY OF THE FIVE FINGERS.

THIS little pig went to market,
This little pig staid at home,
This little pig had a bit of bread and butter,
This little pig had none,
This little pig cried, wee! wee! wee! I can't find my
    way home.

GAMMER GURTON.

A NEW MISTRESS.

CALL me not, love, unkind,
  That from the nunnerie
Of thy chaste heart and quiet mind,
  To war and arms I flie.

Another mistress hence I chace,
  The first foe in the field,
And with a stronger faith embrace
  A sword, a horse, a shield.

LOVELACE.

TO AN EDITOR.

So rude and senseless are thy lays,
  The weary audience vows,
'Tis not the Arcadian swain that sings,
  But 'tis his herd that lows.

SHENSTONE.

IN QUINQUE DIGITOS.

PORCULUS ille forum se contulit ; ille remansit
Usque domi ; panem butyro porculus ille
Perfusum arripuit ; nullum miser ille ; sed 'eheu !'
Ter repetens 'eheu !' clamabat porculus 'eheu !'
Ille, 'ego porcinos nequeo reperire Penates.'

F. H.

NOVUS AMOR.

PARCE precor verbis, cara, indulgere severis,
    Quod de tam casta sede libenter agar,
Sede tuæ mentis tranquillæ in pectore puro,
    Et celer in pugnas et media arma ruam.

Quicunque instructo per campos imperat hosti
    Est novus a nobis ille petendus amor ;
Danda fides clypeo, danda et jam certior ensi,
    Et magis ardentem solicitamus equum.

B. H. D.

AD EDITOREM.

TAM rude carmen habes, ita sunt sine Apolline versus,
    (Pertæsus auditor crepat)
Non est Arcadicus qui cantat arundine pastor,
    Armenta sunt quæ mugiunt.

B.

ELEGY.

THE curfew tolls the knell of parting day,
   The lowing herd winds slowly o'er the lea,
The ploughman homeward plods his weary way,
   And leaves the world to darkness and to me.

Now fades the glimmering landscape on the sight,
   And all the air a solemn stillness holds,
Save where the beetle wheels his droning flight,
   And drowsy tinklings lull the distant folds:

Save that, from yonder ivy-mantled tower,
   The moping owl does to the Moon complain
Of such as, wandering near her secret bower,
   Molest her ancient solitary reign.

Beneath those rugged elms, that yew-tree's shade,
   Where heaves the turf in many a mouldering heap,
Each in his narrow cell for ever laid,
   The rude forefathers of the hamlet sleep.

The breezy call of incense-breathing Morn,
   The swallow twittering from the straw-built shed,
The cock's shrill clarion, or the echoing horn,
   No more shall rouse them from their lowly bed.

For them no more the blazing hearth shall burn,
   Or busy housewife ply her evening care:
No children run to lisp their sire's return,
   Or climb his knees the envied kiss to share.

ELEGIA.

Depositi sonat exequias campana diei,
    Incedit lentum per vaga rura pecus :
Carpit iter, repetitque domum defessus arator,
    Sublustrique moror vespere solus agris.

Nunc oculos fallit species evanida rerum,
    Et passim ætheriæ conticuere plagæ,
Ni rotat argutos qua cantharus aëre gyros,
    Tinnitusque piger sub juga sopit oves.

Ni forte ex hedera vicinæ in vertice turris
    Noctua luctisonos integrat ægra modos,
Si qui palantes latebrosa cubilia propter
    Secreti invadant jura vetusta loci.

Subter nodosis ulmis, taxoque comanti,
    Qua putris aggesto cespite terra tumet,
Cella quisque sua, pagi rudis incola in ævum
    Dormit, et indigenæ contumulantur avi.

Mane in odorifero peramabilis aura Favoni,
    Quæ de straminea garrit hirundo casa,
Argutum galli carmen, lituusve sonorus,
    Discutient humilis somnia nulla tori.

Illis haud iterum refovebitur igne caminus,
    Sponsave quod propriæ est sedula partis aget :
Non balbo proles gratabitur ore parenti,
    Curret in amplexus, præripietve genas.

Oft did the harvest to their sickle yield,
    Their furrow oft the stubborn glebe has broke;
How jocund did they drive their team a-field!
    How bowed the woods beneath their sturdy stroke!

Let not Ambition mock their useful toil,
    Their homely joys, and destiny obscure;
Nor Grandeur hear with a disdainful smile,
    The short and simple annals of the poor.

The boast of heraldry, the pomp of power,
    And all that beauty, all that wealth e'er gave,
Await alike th' inevitable hour:
    The paths of glory lead but to the grave.

Nor you, ye proud, impute to these the fault,
    If Memory o'er their tomb no trophies raise,
Where through the long drawn aisle and fretted vault,
    The pealing anthem swells the note of praise.

Can storied urn or animated bust
    Back to its mansion call the fleeting breath?
Can Honour's voice provoke the silent dust,
    Or Flattery soothe the dull cold ear of Death?

Perhaps in this neglected spot is laid
    Some heart once pregnant with celestial fire;
Hands, that the rod of empire might have swayed,
    Or waked to ecstasy the living lyre.

Suppositis quoties resecabant falcibus arva,
  Scissa gravi quoties vomere gleba fuit :
Ut læti in tonsas jumenta egere novales,
  Quo ferro in sylvis procubuere trabes !

Ambitio curas ne dedignetur honestas,
  Otiaque ignotis haud aliena focis ;
Nec torvo excipiat contracta Superbia risu
  Pauperis historiam, sit brevis illa, domi.

Stemmata longa patrum, magnæque potentia famæ,
  Quicquid forma potest addere, quicquid opes,
Expectant pariter non evitabile tempus—
  Scilicet ad tumulum ducit Honoris iter.

Nec vos, o proceres phalerati, id vertite culpæ,
  Quod Pietas illis nulla tropæa locat,
Qua per magnifici laquearia dædala templi
  Grandisonum volvunt organa pulsa melos.

Quid tituli, quid sculpta juvabunt marmora? membris
  An sese insinuet spiritus arte redux?
Gloria num tacitas exsuscitet ore favillas?
  Num Stygium tangant mollia verba Deum?

Forsitan hac etiam neglecta in sede quiescant
  Quæ cœlo fuerant pectora fœta suo ;
Dextera, quæ indomitos domuisset inulta Britannos,
  Vel poterat vivam solicitasse lyram.

But Knowledge to their eyes her ample page,
  Rich with the spoils of time, did ne'er unroll;
Chill Penury repressed their noble rage,
  And froze the genial current of the soul.

Full many a gem of purest ray serene,
  The dark unfathomed caves of ocean bear:
Full many a flower is born to blush unseen,
  And waste its sweetness on the desert air.

Some village-Hampden, that with dauntless breast
  The little tyrant of his fields withstood;
Some mute inglorious Milton here may rest,
  Some Cromwell guiltless of his country's blood.

Th' applause of listening senates to command,
  The threats of pain and ruin to despise,
To scatter plenty o'er a smiling land,
  And read their history in a nation's eyes,

Their lot forbad: nor circumscribed alone
  Their growing virtues, but their crimes confined;
Forbad to wade through slaughter to a throne,
  And shut the gates of mercy on mankind;

The struggling pangs of conscious truth to hide,
  To quench the blushes of ingenuous shame,
Or heap the shrine of Luxury and Pride
  With incense kindled at the Muse's flame.

Atqui non illis rerum monumenta, nec amplas
　　Temporis exuvias evoluisse datur :
Frigida Paupertas generosos expulit ignes,
　　Compressitque pigro corda animosque gelu.

Plurima, quæ raro splendet fulgore, sub imis
　　Fontibus oceani gemma sepulta latet :
Plurimus incultis nequicquam nascitur arvis
　　Flosculus, et vacuum complet odore nemus.

Hac, indignatus ruris dare colla tyranno,
　　Brutus in obscura dormiat alter humo ;
Inscius hic citharæ Nasoque inglorius ævi,
　　Nec patriæ temerans fœdera Cæsar aquæ.

Imperitare animo pendentis ab ore senatus,
　　Temnere pænarum damna gravesque minas,
Per gentes pleno diffundere munera cornu,
　　Et scribi in populi vultubus urbis amor,

Sorte negatum illis—nec, quæ virtutibus essent
　　Invida, nequitiæ Fata dedere viam :
Sed vetuere armis male parta capessere regna,
　　Et generi exitium deproperare suo ;

Condere sinceros agitato in pectore motus,
　　Luctari ingenuus ne rubor ora notet,
Aut ferre ad tumidi cumulata altaria luxus
　　Pro pudor ! Aonii thurea dona chori.

Far from the madding crowd's ignoble strife,
  Their sober wishes never learned to stray;
Along the cool sequestered vale of life
  They kept the noiseless tenour of their way.

Yet e'en these bones from insult to protect,
  Some frail memorial still erected nigh,
With uncouth rhymes and shapeless sculpture decked,
  Implores the passing tribute of a sigh.

Their name, their years, spelt by th' unlettered Muse,
  The place of fame and elegy supply:
And many a holy text around she strews,
  That teach the rustic moralist to die.

For who, to dumb Forgetfulness a prey,
  This pleasing anxious being e'er resigned,
Left the warm precincts of the cheerful day,
  Nor cast one longing, lingering look behind?

On some fond breast the parting soul relies,
  Some pious drops the closing eye requires;
E'en from the tomb the voice of Nature cries,
  E'en in our ashes live their wonted fires.

For thee, who, mindful of th' unhonoured dead,
  Dost in these lines their artless tale relate;
If chance, by lonely Contemplation led,
  Some kindred spirit shall inquire thy fate,

Ambitione procul vesana et lite forensi,
  Quisque suum placide conficiebat iter :
Per vitæ ambages gratas in valle reducta
  Carpebant tacitos ac sine labe dies.

Hæc tamen ut pedibus sint ossa intacta profanis,
  E fragili saxo tollitur urna memor,
Quæ versu illepido sculptisque sine arte figuris
  Sæpe viatorem sistere, flere monet.

Musa rudis signat quæ nomina, computat annos,
  Quicquid laudis egent suppeditare valet ;
Aureaque excerpsit sacrato e codice dicta,
  Quæ doceant quid sit vivere, quidque mori.

Nam quis pervigilis, sic immemor usque priorum,
  Delicias animæ deposuisse velit ?
Ecquis deseruit lætæ confinia lucis,
  Nec tulit ad superas ora reflexa plagas ?

Sese anima in gremium fugitiva receptat amicum,
  Ultima lachrymulam flagitat hora piam :
Vel de ferali clamat Natura sepulchro,
  Vel calet effœto fax rediviva rogo !

Te vero, memorem turbæ sine honore jacentis,
  Quem juvat infletas sic retulisse vices,
Si te forte dolens, animo huc compulsus eodem,
  Advena, quæ fuerint et tua fata, petat :

Haply some hoary-headed swain may say,
  ' Oft have we seen him at the peep of dawn
Brushing with hasty steps the dews away
  To meet the sun upon the upland lawn.

There at the foot of yonder nodding beech,
  That wreathes its old fantastic roots so high,
His listless length at noontide would he stretch,
  And pore upon the brook that babbles by.

Hard by yon wood, now smiling as in scorn,
  Muttering his wayward fancies he would rove,
Now drooping woeful wan, like one forlorn,
  Or crazed with care, or crossed in hopeless love.

One morn I missed him on the 'customed hill,
  Along the heath and near his favourite tree;
Another came; nor yet beside the rill,
  Nor up the lawn, nor at the wood was he:

The next with dirges due in sad array
  Slow through the church-way path we saw him borne.
Approach and read (for thou canst read) the lay,
  Graved on the stone beneath yon aged thorn.'

THE EPITAPH.

Here rests his head upon the lap of Earth,
  A youth to fortune and to fame unknown,
Fair Science frowned not on his humble birth,
  And Melancholy marked him for her own.

Dixerit, albescant cana cui fronte capilli;
  ' Mane novo juvenis sæpe videndus erat,
Cum pede festino quateret de gramine rores,
  Staret ut in summis, sole oriente, jugis.

Illic qua fagi patet umbra, vetustaque radix
  Lascive e summa tortilis exstat humo,
Sole sub æstivo molli porrectus in herba
  Captabat murmur lene loquacis aquæ.

Ad nemus ille vagans, risuque notandus amaro,
  Mussabat dubios, intima corda, sonos:
Vel miser et pallens sese incomitatus agebat,
  Deliro similis, quemve fefellit amor.

Mane mihi quodam collis juga nota petenti
  Arboris et soliti defuit hospes agri:
Altera lux oritur—nec propter flumen, aprico
  Nec tamen in campo, nec nemora inter, erat.

Tertia successit—planctus audimus—et inde
  Funeris elati triste notamus iter.
Perlege (namque potes) tumulo superaddita verba,
  Surgit sub vetulo qua lapis ille rubo.'

EPITAPHIUM.

Hic recubat juvenis maternæ in cespite terræ;
  Fama latet—nullas vivus habebat opes.
Hunc placido vidit nascentem lumine Musa,
  Et puerum optavit lugubris Hora suum.

Large was his bounty, and his soul sincere,
 Heaven did a recompence as largely send:
He gave to Misery all he had—a tear;
 He gained from Heaven—'twas all he wished—a friend.

No further seek his merits to disclose,
 Or draw his frailties from their dread abode,
There they alike in trembling hope repose,
 The bosom of his Father and his God.

GRAY.

ENOUGH'S A FEAST.

I WENT to the toad that lies under the wall,
I charmed him out, and he came at my call:
I scratched out the eyes of the owl before;
I tore the bat's wing—what would you have more?

THUS EVER.

OH! ever thus, from childhood's hour,
 I've seen my fondest hopes decay;
I never loved a tree or flower,
 But 'twas the first to fade away.
I never nursed a dear gazelle,
 To glad me with its soft black eye,
But when it came to know me well,
 And love me, it was sure to die.

MOORE.

Ipse animi simplex largi, quæ reddidit ultro
  Largior, agnovit libera dona, Deus :
Pauper pauperibus lacrymam, munuscula, fudit,
  Ex voto Cœli nactus amicitiam.

Sed neque virtutes evolvere longius illas,
  Nec vitia a tenebris dissociare velis :
Spe pariter tacita, pariter terrore quiescunt,
  In Patris æterno non adeunda sinu.

J. H. M.

SATIS SUPERQUE.

Bufonem accessi sub pariete semper agentem,
  Vocibus elicui magicis, venitque vocatus :
Alam divelli vespertilionis, ocellis
  Privato bubone prius—quid plura requiras ?

F. H.

SIC SEMPER.

Sic mihi de teneris spes infeliciter annis,
  Et vota et cupidæ præteriere preces !
Arbusta in sylvis, in aprico flosculus horto—
  Sub manibus pereunt omnia pulcra meis.
Si forte effusi mirantem fulgur ocelli,
  Jam me surpuerat cara capella mihi,
Cum sciret vocem, peteret mea basia, mecum
  Luderet—ad certam mittitur illa necem !

H. D.

THE MAN IN THE WILDERNESS.

THE man in the wilderness asked me,
' How many strawberries grow in the sea?'
I answered him, as I thought good,
' As many as red herrings grow in the wood.'

GAMMER GURTON.

EPISTLE TO A FRIEND.

WELL, be it so, my friend!—I've done
With mirth, extravagance and fun:
I fear I've passed the fatal line:
That unchecked mirth and unstopped wine,
That flow of wit that knows no bound,
The merry laugh's perpetual round,
Nay, e'en the social generous glow
That all-enlivening grapes bestow—
Joys that a few brief sennights past
I thought eternally would last,
Or fondly wished, before they fled,
I might be numbered with the dead—
No more are tricked with charms for me,
Nor wake my soul to jollity:
That if to pleasure I incline,
No more I view her form in wine,
Nor if bleak care besets my soul,
Can drown him in the sparkling bowl.

QUIDAM IN DESERTIS.

QUIDAM in desertis blanda me voce rogavit,
  'Fraga quot in pelagi fluctibus orta putes?'
Nec male quæsitis hoc respondere videbar,
  'Salsa quot alecum millia sylva ferat.'

F. H.

AD AMICUM.

DIXTI heu! omnia vera, mi sodalis!
Bacchanalia nostra terminavi,
Cum vino et sale et omnibus cachinnis.
Fervens ille lepos, fluensque vinum,
Mollis circuitus facetiarum,
Et risus hilares, jocique belli;
Imo, omnis generosa vis Lyæi,
Seu quid suavius est elegantiusque,
Quod vivax dedit uva dissolutis—
Quales blanditias prius putabam
Orturas magis in dies et horas,
Aut ante expetii ipse, quam perirent,
Convivas numerarer inter Orci—
Cuncta hæc illecebris carent, nec udæ
Incendunt animæ protervitatem;
Sed sive Euphrosynem peto jocosam,
Non inter calices, ut ante, ridet;
Nec si Cura sinum maligna torquet,
Mergenda est cyathi scatentis æstu.

Farewell, farewell, delusive dream!

The joy of youth, the poet's theme;

Enchanting scenes of mirth and glee,

When all was gay and all was free;

When infant love's first sparks were fanned,

Cemented friendship's strictest band,

And both together bore along

In union sweet the power of song.

Enchanting scenes, that fancy loves,

That friendship's sacred voice approves;

On which remembrance oft shall dwell

With sad delight—dear scenes, farewell!

  Even so, I've passed the fatal line,

And other suns upon me shine:

But as the home-sick sailor sees

Mid the waste waves his native trees;

And thinks the wide-stretched watery scene

Fair meadows clad in vernal green:

So oft my fancy turns to view

Those forms my livelier moments knew,

Actum est: desinimus levis juventæ
Vatum et delicias inaniorum,
Ah quam somnia grata, somniare!
O dulces aditus, dies amœni,
Noctes aureolæ, mihi valete,
Quum festum fuit omne liberumque;
Quando infans amor arsit in medullis,
Juncti fœderibus piis amici,
Et quicquid leve fulsit aut venustum
Dilectæ harmoniam lyræ docebat!
Quas non perdite amare mens recusat,
Nec voces comitum sacræ tacebunt,
Cordi quæ memori diu recurrent,
Ut solatiolum mei laboris,
O horæ ambrosiæ, mihi valete!

    Dixti heu! omnia vera, mi sodalis—
Bacchanalia nostra terminavi,
Et soles alios tepere sensi.
Sed vasto veluti in maris profundo
Fessus nauta videt nemus paternum,
Pingitque in vitreis fretis aquarum
Verni pascua ruris atque flores:
Sic rerum mihi pertinax imago
Et desiderium redit priorum,
Quas in purpureis sequebar annis.

And kindling at delusions vain,
Believes and hopes them back again.
Then if I court their imaged charms,
My fevered soul is up in arms;
And sickening nature proves at last
The passion weak, the moment past.

MERIVALE.

THE MAN OF THESSALY.

THERE was a man of Thessaly,
  And he was wondrous wise;
He jumped into a quickset hedge
  And scratched out both his eyes:
And when he saw his eyes were out,
  With all his might and main
He jumped into another hedge—
  And scratched them in again.

GAMMER GURTON.

Et priscos foveo arroganter ignes,
Credoque esse meos, libensque fallor.
Quod si jam simulacra læta capto,
Menti nescio quid febriculosæ
Certatim irruit, et pudet fateri
Quam vini levis avolet libido,
Quam fallax rosa, quam brevis juventus!

H. D.

VIR THESSALICUS.

Ἐξ οὐ τυχόντων Θέτταλός τις ἦν ἀνήρ,
ὃς ἔργον ἐπεχείρησε τλημονέστατον·
ἀκανθοχηνοκοκκόβατον εἰσήλατο,
δίσσας τ᾽ ἀνεξώρυξεν ὀφθάλμων κόρας.
ὡς οὖν τὰ πραχθέντ᾽ ἔβλεπεν τυφλὸς γεγώς,
οὐ μὴν ὑπέπτηξ᾽ οὐδέν, ἀλλ᾽ εὐκαρδίως
βάτον τιν᾽ ἄλλην ἥλατ᾽ εἰς ἀκανθίνην,
κἀκ τοῦδ᾽ ἐγένετ᾽ ἐξαῦθις ἐκ τυφλοῦ βλέπων.

S. B.

Thessalus acer erat sapiens præ civibus unus,
Qui mediam insiluit spineta per horrida sepem,
Effoditque oculos sibi crudelissimus ambos.
Cum vero effossos orbes sine lumine vidit,
Viribus enisum totis illum altera sepes
Accipit, et raptos oculos cito reddit egenti.

F. H.

THIS INTRODUCETH TO MIE LIBRARIE.

From moulderinge Abbayes' darke Scriptorium broughte
See vellum tomes by monkysh laboure wroughte;
Ne yette the Comma borne, Papyri see,
And uncial letterres' wizarde grammarie.
View mie Fyfthteeneres in their ruggedde line;
Swylke Inkes! swylke Linnenne! only knowne longe syne—
Enteringe, where Aldus mote have fixt his throne,
Or Harrie Stevenes covetedde his owne.

Drurie.

IN MUSÆI . MEI . ADITU.

PONTIFICUM . VIDEAS . PENETRALIBUS . ERUTA . LABSIS

ANTIQUAS . MONACHUM . VELLERA . PASSA . MANUS

ET . VETERES . PUNCTO . SINE . DIVISORE . PAPYROS

QUÆQUE . FREMIT . MONSTRIS . LITERA . PICTA . SUIS

ÆTATIS . DECIMÆ . SPECTES . INDUSTRIA . QUINTÆ

QUAM . PULCRA . ARCHETYPOS . IMPRIMAT . ARTE . DUCES

ALDINAS . ÆDES . INEUNS . ET . LIMINA . JUNTÆ

QUOSQUE . SUOS . STEPHANUS . VELLET . HABERE . LARES

H. J. T. D.

PRECEDENCE.

' Sir, will you please to walk before?'
' No pray, Sir, you are next the door:'
' Upon my honour, I'll not stir'—
' Sir, I'm at home—consider, Sir!'
' Excuse me Sir, I'll not go first:'
' Well if I must be rude, I must—
But yet I wish I could evade it;
'Tis strangely clownish—be persuaded.'
 Go forward cits—go forward squires;
Nor scruple each what each admires.
Life squares not friends with your proceeding,
It flies while you display your breeding:
Such breeding as one's grannam preaches,
Or some old dancing master teaches.
O for some rude tumultuous fellow,
Half crazy, or at least half mellow,
To come behind you unawares
And fairly kick you both down stairs!
 But, Death's at hand—let me advise ye,
Go forward friends, or he'll surprise ye.

SHENSTONE.

THE QUIET OLD LADY.

THERE was an old woman lived under a hill,
And if she's not gone, she lives there still.

GAMMER GURTON.

PRÆCEDERE.

'I PRÆ, pone sequar, Domine'—'haud præcedere possum'–
'I prece te rogito: foribus quin proximus adstas!'
'Juro Phœbeos crines, pede figor'—'at hæc est
Nostra domus, reputa'—'Veniam da, non prior ibo!'
'Quam sit inurbanum novi, at parere necesse est;
Longe aliter facerem—precor O succumbe roganti.'
   Ite, præite aliis alii, vos quotquot ab urbe,
Armigeri quotquot proceres de rure: nec id quod
Pectore amat toto, sibi quisque assumere nolit.
Vita brevis male se vestris accommodat hisce
Usubus; illa fugit, dum vos ornatis ad unguem
Exhibitos mores, quales docuisset ineptæ
Garrulitas aviæ, aut balbi præcepta Bathylli.
Asper et incultus veniat quis, sit simul idem
Ebriolus, paulum aut demens, qui calce faceto
Urgens de tergo, scalas abscondere cogat.
   Sed quid ego plura? En præsto stat Mors! nisi vultis
Ire, hæc attonitos protrudet et ire negantes.

B.

ANUS TRANQUILLA.

LEGIT Anus sub colle domum: domus illa morantem,
  Si non ipsa abeat, jam retinebit anum.

F. H.

THE BUD.

LATELY on yonder swelling bush,
  Big with many a coming rose,
This early bud began to blush,
  And did but half itself disclose :
I plucked it, though no better grown ;
And now you see how full 'tis blown.

Still as I did the leaves inspire,
  With such a purple light they shone,
As if they had been made of fire,
  And spreading so would flame anon.
All that was meant by air and sun
To the young flower, my breath has done.

If our loose breath so much can do,
  What may the same in forms of love,
Of purest love and music too,
  When Flavia it aspires to move?
When that, which lifeless buds persuades
To wax more soft, her youth invades?

WALLER.

HARRY'S CALF.

' HARRY, I cannot think,' says Dick,
' What makes your ancles grow so thick ;'
' You do not recollect,' says Harry,
' What a great calf they have to carry !'

PRIOR.

GEMMA.

En !—ea qua foliis stet operta recentibus arbor
  Et properet gravidas mox aperire rosas—
Hæc præmaturi prope conscia gemma ruboris
  Intempestivum est pandere visa caput.
Hanc ego, sicut erat, summo de stemmate vulsi,
  Jamque patent teneræ quæ latuere comæ.

Et quoties tepido caluit rosa percita flatu,
  Purpura per nitidas fulsit oborta genas;
Ac veluti admotis auris caluere favillæ,
  Afflatæ visa est ignea forma rosæ.
Vis adeo solis faceret quod et ala Favoni,
  Hoc datur exiguo flamine posse mihi.

Talia si possit nostri temere halitus oris,
  Idem quid tenero non in amore potest?
Purus amor quoties citharæ se commodet arti,
  Et tremat assiduis Flavia mota labris?
Cum, domat exanimes qui sub juga mollia gemmas,
  Virgineum expugnet spiritus ille sinum?

                                        J. H.

DAVUS VITULINUS.

'Non potest, Dave, excogitari
  Cur sis tam crassus in talari?'
'Sis memor'—huic respondet Davus—
'Quam vitulus vehendus gravis!'

                                        B.

THE FIRST GRIEF.

' OH call my brother back to me,
  I cannot play alone:
The summer comes with flower and bee—
  Where is my brother gone?

The butterfly is glancing bright
  Along the sunbeam's track;
I care not now to chase its flight—
  O call my brother back.

The flowers run wild—the flowers we sowed
  Around our garden tree;
Our vine is drooping with its load—
  O call him back to me!'

' He would not hear my voice, fair child;
  He may not come to thee:
The face, that once like spring-time smiled,
  On earth no more thou'lt see.

A flower's brief bright life of joy,
  Such unto him was given:
Go, thou must play alone my boy—
  Thy brother is in heaven.'

PRIMUS DOLOR.

'O REVOCA mihi fratrem, et eris carissima, mater;
  Solus enim nequeo ludere, fessus ero.
Cum pictis apibus, venit cum floribus æstas—
  Dic quibus in cæcis abditur ille locis?

Trans jubar aurati volitans mutabile solis
  Ala papilio versicolore micat;
Et micet incolumis; per me volitabit inultus—
  O redeat nostram frater, ut ante, domum!

Intonsi exultant flores—quem sevimus hortum;
  Arbore sub patula quæ rubuere rosæ:
Vitis dependet crassis onerata racemis—
  Si revocas fratrem, tu mihi mater eris.'

'Heu! non audiret matrem, formose, vocantem,
  Quem poterunt nullæ solicitare preces:
Ille oculus ridens, faciesque simillima veri,
  Et nos et nostrum destituere diem.

Sole sub aprico quid si breve carpserit ævum?
  Splendida decidui tempora floris habet.
I, puer—et ludos tecum meditare novellos;
  Nec geme quod cœlis gaudeat ille suis.'

' And has he left the birds and flowers,
   And must I call in vain?
And through the long long 'summer hours
   Will he not come again?

And by the brook and in the glade
   Are all our wanderings o'er?
O! while my brother with me played
   Would I had loved him more!'

HEMANS.

FIDELE'S GRAVE.

WITH fairest flowers,

Whilst summer lasts, and I live here, Fidele,
I'll sweeten thy sad grave: thou shalt not lack
The flower, that's like thy face, pale primrose; nor
The azure harebell, like thy veins; no, nor
The leaf of eglantine, which not to slander,
Out-sweetened not thy breath: the ruddock would,
With charitable bill (O bill, sore shaming
Those rich left heirs, that let their fathers lie
Without a monument!) bring thee all this;
Yea, and furred moss beside, when flowers are none,
To winter-ground thy corse.

SHAKESPEARE.

' Ergo abit, et volucres et gemmea prata reliquit?
Et mea nequicquam vox repetita sonat?
Immemor et nostri, per tœdia longa dierum,
Per totam æstatem non venit usque mihi?

Nec rursum in viridi reduces errabimus umbra?
Ad nemus, ad fontes, incomitatus eam?
Dure puer, qui tot dulces neglexeris horas,
Nec dederis fratri basia plura tuo!'

H. D.

FIDELES TUMULUS.

Tuum, Fidele, floribus pulcerrimis,
Dum durat æstas, incolamque me vident
Hæc rura, funus contegam : pallentium,
Tui instar oris, primularum copia
Haud deerit, aut colore venas æmulans
Hyacinthus, aut odora frons cynosbati :
Quæ, nec calumniamur, haud erat tuo,
Odora quamvis, spiritu fragrantior.
Tibi hæc vetustæ more mansuetudinis
(O mos pudori prodigis hæredibus
Inhumata patrum qui relinquunt corpora!)
Rubecularum vilis hospitalitas
Afferret; imo plura; namque mortuis
His omnibus, cubile musco sterneret,
Brumaque te curaret, ut viresceres.

F. H.

TO CERES.

Ceres, most bounteous lady, thy rich leas
Of wheat, rye, barley, vetches, oats and pease;
Thy turfy mountains, where live nibbling sheep,
And flat meads thatched with stover, them to keep:
Thy bank with pionied and twilled brims,
Which spungy April at thy hest betrims,
To make cold nymphs chaste crowns; and thy broom
    groves,
Whose shadow the dismissed bachelor loves,
Being lass-lorn; thy pole clipt vineyard;
And thy sea-marge sterile and rocky-hard,
Where thou thyself dost air—the queen o' the sky,
Whose watery arch, and messenger am I,
Bids thee leave these; and with her sovereign grace,
Here on this grass-plot, in this very place,
To come and sport: her peacocks fly amain;
Approach, rich Ceres, her to entertain.

                    SHAKESPEARE.

CHARLEY.

Charley loves good ale and wine,
  And Charley loves good brandy,
And Charley loves a pretty girl,
  As sweet as sugar candy.

                    GAMMER GURTON.

AD CEREREM.

Diva Ceres, opulenta, tibi hæc Junonia longe
Jussa fero, cujus liquidis in nubibus Iris
Ipsa per ætherios labor prænuntia tractus.
Jamne tuas multa vibrantes messe novales,
Triticeamque ultro segetem, viciamque, fabamque,
Linquis, et erectæ penetrabile culmen avenæ?
Jamne tuos montes, ovium et rodentia sæcla,
Et, tutela vagi pecoris, quæ plurima sepes
Implicitis planos distinxit cratibus agros?
Jamne et ripicolas fluviorum in margine flores,
Lilia, pæoniamque, Aprilia dona, rubentem,
Usum in nympharum, et nuribus redimicula castis?
At neque te multo vindemia consita palo,
Quæque genistarum læsis stat amantibus umbra,
Detineat; nec litus iners scruposaque saxa,
Æquoris in scatebris ubi mollia frigora captas.
Sic Regina jubet, tecum hæc viridaria ludo
Quæ terere et dulces dignatur inire choreas.
At bijugis actos pavonibus aspice currus!
Ipsa veni, Dominamque pio, Diva, accipe vultu.

C. M.

CAROLI DELICIÆ.

Carolus acer amat cerevisia vina, merumque
    Carolus, et quotquot fortia et uda simul;
Carolus egregiam formosa fronte puellam,
    Et dulcem, ut succus quem sua canna parit.

F. H.

EVENING.

HAIL meek eyed maiden, clad in sober grey,
  Whose soft approach the weary woodman loves,
As homeward bent to kiss his prattling babes,
  Jocund he whistles through the twilight groves.

When Phœbus sinks behind the gilded hills,
  You lightly o'er the misty meadows walk ;
The drooping daisies bathe in honey dews,
  And nurse the nodding violet's tender stalk.

The panting Dryads that in day's fierce heat
  To inmost bowers and cooling caverns ran,
Return to trip in wanton evening dance ;
  Old Silvan too returns, and laughing Pan.

To the deep wood the clamorous rooks repair,
  Light skims the swallow o'er the watery scene ;
And from the sheep-cote and fresh furrowed field
  Stout ploughmen meet, to wrestle on the green.

The swain, that artless sings on yonder rock,
  His supping sheep and lengthening shadow spies ;
Pleased with the cool, the calm, refreshful hour,
  And with hoarse humming of unnumbered flies.

VESPERA.

Te placido vultu glaucaque in veste, Puella,
    Leniter ingressam fessus arator amat :
Ille domum repetens balbæ parat oscula proli,
    Et nemorum tenebris omnia læta canit.

Cum sub purpureos condit sol lumina montes,
    Tu levis incedens prata vapore tegis,
Lilia mellifero perfundis rore per herbam,
    Nutantem violam tu fragilemque foves.

Quæ Dryades trepidæ fugerunt solis anheli
    Spelunca in tacita vim gelidoque cavo,
Lasciva properant reduces saltare chorea,
    Pan quoque Silvano cum sene festus adest.

Ecce ! lacus placidos circumvolat ales hirundo,
    Cornices siluas, garrula turba, petunt ;
A grege composito sulcoque recente coloni
    Certatum in viridi congrediuntur humo.

Aspicit exercens pastor sine lege Camœnam,
    Cœnantum ut pecudum longior umbra cadat ;
Illum etiam gelidi tranquilla silentia mulcent
    Temporis, et rauco plurima musca sono.

Now every passion sleeps; desponding Love,
    And pining Envy, ever-restless Pride;
A holy calm creeps o'er my peaceful soul,
    Anger and mad Ambition's storms subside.

O modest Evening! oft let me appear
    A wandering votary in thy pensive train;
Listening to every wildly-warbling throat
    That fills with farewell sweet thy darkening plain.
                                   ANON.

FROM THE ORIGINAL OPPOSITE.

SING a song of sixpence,
    A pocket full of rye;
Four and twenty blackbirds
    Baked in a pie:
When the pie was opened
    The birds began to sing;
Was not that a dainty dish
    To set before the King?

The King was in the parlour
    Counting out his money;
The Queen was in the kitchen
    Eating bread and honey;
The maid was in the garden
    Hanging out the clothes:
Down came a blackbird
    And carried off her nose.
                          GAMMER GURTON.

Nunc posuere animi ; nunc ægra Superbia dormit,
  Invidiæque Dolor, speque relictus Amor ;
Fundit sancta quies optatam in pectora pacem ;
  Spes nimiæ fugiunt, nec levis Ira tumet.

Sit mihi, sit tecum meditanti errare per agros ;
  Me, virgo, sociis adde modesta tuis :
Sit mihi sæpe vaga volucrum gaudere querela,
  Quæ tua, dum recinit, personat arva—vale !

L.

Athenæi Fragmentum in palimpsestis bibliothecæ Ambrosianæ ab Angelo
Maio inventum, hactenus vero non editum.

— περὶ δὲ τῶν κοσσύφων, ὡς ἐκ κριβάνων τοῖς
δειπνοῦσι παρατεθέντα ᾄδουσι, περὶ δὲ τῶν στρουθίων,
ὡς τῶν παιδισκῶν τὰς ῥῖνας καθιπτάμενα ἁρπάζει,
τῶν κωμικῶν τις οὕτως γράφει·

ἎΙσμα νῦν τετρωβολαῖον, ᾄδετ᾽, ἄνδρες δημόται,
καννάβου τίς ἐστ᾽ ἐν οἴκῳ θύλακος ζεῶν πλέως,
κοσσύφων δὲ κριβανιτῶν τετράδι ἓξ ἐν πέμματι·
πέμμα δ᾽ ὡς ἤνοιξε δαιτρός, ὡς ἔμελψαν κόσσυφοι·
οὐ τόδ᾽ ἦν ἔδεσμα δείπνοις τοῖς τυραννικοῖς πρέπον ;
ἐν τρικλινίῳ τύραννος κολλυβίστης ἕζετο,
ἕζετ᾽ ἀναβάδην τυράννη γ᾽· ἄρτον ἠδὲ καὶ μέλι
ἤσθιεν· κόρη δ᾽ ἐν αὐλαῖς ἐκρέμασε τὰ βύσσινα,
νηπία· τέγους γὰρ εὐθὺ στρουθίον καθηλμένον
εἶτα ῥῖνα τῆς ταλαίνης ᾤχετ᾽ ἐν ῥύγχῳ φέρον.

E. C. H.

THE OLD ARM-CHAIR.

I LOVE it, I love it, and who shall dare
To chide me for loving that old Arm-Chair?
I've treasured it long as a sainted prize;
I've bedewed it with tears and embalmed it with sighs:
'Tis bound by a thousand bands to my heart,
Not a tie will break, not a link will start:
Would ye know the spell?—a Mother sat there,
And a sacred thing is that old Arm-Chair.

In childhood's hour I lingered near
The hallowed seat with listening ear;
And gentle words that mother would give
To fit me to die and teach me to live.
She told me shame would never betide
With truth to my creed and God for my guide;
She taught me to lisp my earliest prayer,
As I knelt beside that old Arm-Chair.

I sat and watched her many a day,
While her eyes grew dim and her locks were grey;
And I almost worshipped her when she smiled,
And turned from the Bible to bless her child.
Years rolled on—but the last one sped;
My idol was shattered, my earth star fled;
I learnt how much the soul can bear—
When I saw her die in the old Arm-Chair.

CATHEDRA VETUS.

Illam amo, quantum amo! Invidus taceat,
Si mihi vetus hæc Cathedra placeat.
Illam præ mercibus condidi Tyriis,
Lacrymis sparsi, fudi suspiriis:
Illa adamantino stringitur cordi
Nexu et vinculo—scilicet audi:
Sedit in illa heu! matrum tenerrima;
Et vetus hæc Cathedra est rerum sacerrima.

Hanc prope sedem puer cunctabar,
Imbibens vocem quam venerabar;
Matris ego hauriens verba moventia,
Et bene vivere et mori docentia:
Illa docebat, quam minime puduit,
Si veritati quis et Deo studuit;
Donec flectebam cum prece strenua
Ad latus veteris Cathedræ genua.

Quantum invigilavi, et totus in illis,
Nocti oculorum et canis capillis!
Quam Deam putavi, cum illa ridebat,
Deam esse, pro puero cum supplicabat!
Sed anni—ah! ultimus annus præteriit,
Meus amor excessit et lux mea periit:
De carcere luctus ad metam percurritur,
Quando illa in veteri Cathedra moritur.

'Tis past, 'tis past—but I gaze on it now
With aching heart and throbbing brow:
'Twas there she nursed me, and there she died:
And memory flows with a lava tide.
Say it is folly and deem me weak,
Whilst the scalding drops roll down my cheek;
But I love it, I love it, and cannot tear
My soul from my Mother's old Arm-Chair.

E. COOKE.

SHE THAT LIVED IN A SHOE.

THERE was an old woman who lived in a shoe;
She had so many children she did'nt know what to do.
She gave them some broth without any bread,
Then whipt them all soundly and sent them to bed.

GAMMER GURTON.

BE WISE AND LIVE.

HE who fights and runs away
Will live to fight another day;
But he who is in battle slain
Can never hope to fight again.

BUTLER.

Abiit, abiit!—sed reminiscimur,
Tremuli, mœsti: en sedes ipsissima!
Illa me fovit et occidit illa;
Redeunt animo tristia mille.
Sinam stultitiæ meæ moneri,
Ignea gutta non vult cohiberi.
Illam amo, quantum amo!—rideant cæteri;
Matris ego immorer Cathedræ veteri!

H. D.

ANUS IN SOLEA.

ANXIA vixit anus, solea conclusa minuta,
Pressaque tot pueris et nescia quid sit agendum;
Jus illis tepidum quæ cum sine pane parasset,
Sæva flagellavit cunctos, cubitumque remisit.

F. H.

SAPERE ET VIVERE.

QUI pugnans parmam jacit et post terga reliquit,
Ille potest alio prœlia inire die:
At bello qui cæsus humum semel ore momordit,
Post ea non ullo Marte notandus erit.

B.

THE SHRUBBERY.

Oh! happy shades—to me unblest!
  Friendly to peace, but not to me!
How ill the scene that offers rest,
  And hearts that cannot rest, agree!

This glassy stream, that spreading pine,
  Those alders quivering to the breeze,
Might soothe a soul less hurt than mine,
  And please, if anything could please.

But fixed unalterable Care
  Forgoes not what she feels within,
Shews the same sadness every where,
  And slights the season and the scene.

For all that pleased in wood or lawn,
  While peace possessed those silent bowers;
Her animating smile withdrawn,
  Has lost its beauties and its powers.

The saint or moralist should tread
  This moss grown alley musing, slow;
They seek like me the secret shade,
  But not like me to nourish woe!

Me fruitful scenes and prospects waste
  Alike admonish not to roam;
These tell me of enjoyments past,
  And those of sorrows yet to come.

Cowper.

FRUTETUM.

Vos, O felices umbræ, mihi gaudia nulla
  Præbetis, quamvis vos amet ipsa quies:
Quam male conveniunt cor quod requiescere nescit,
  Et locus ignavæ deditus ille moræ!

Hic vitro fons lucidior, proceraque pinus,
  Et salices illæ quas levis aura movet,
Forte minus læsæ referant solatia menti,
  Et me, si valeant ulla juvare, juvent.

Sed vultu torvo, implacidis quæ surdior Euris,
  Non sinit expelli Cura quod intus habet;
Illam atri sequitur facies tristissima cœli,
  Immemorem pariter temporis atque loci.

Quicquid enim in foliis viridique placebat in herba,
  Et rura et tacitum pace tenente nemus,
Abrepto risu, qui rerum inspirat amorem,
  Undique delicias perdidit omne suas.

Hac in muscosa, qui vero innititur, umbra
  Cogitet arcani mystica jura Dei;
Ille amat et silvas, sed non ut pabula luctus
  Concipiat, similis dissimilisque mei.

Me fœcundus ager simul et deserta ferarum,
  Deserere has sedes et loca nota vetant:
Alter præteritos memorat felicius annos;
  Altera, venturi quod dabit hora mali.

J. M.

ALCESTIS.

Ἐγὼ καὶ διὰ Μούσας,
καὶ μετάρσιος ἦξα, καὶ
πλεῖστον ἀψάμενος λόγον
κρεῖσσον οὐδὲν Ἀνάγκας
εὗρον· οὐδέ τι φάρμακον
Θρήσσαις ἐν σανίσι, τὰς
Ὀρφεία κατέγραψε
γῆρυς· οὐδ᾽ ὅσα Φοῖβος
Ἀσκληπιαδίασιν παρέδωκε
φάρμακα πολυπόνοις
ἀντιτεμὼν βροτοῖσι.

Ἀντ. ά.
μόνας δ᾽ οὔτ᾽ ἐπὶ βωμοὺς
ἐλθεῖν οὔτε βρέτας θεᾶς
ἐστὶν, οὐ σφαγίων κλύει.
μή μοι, πότνια, μείζων
ἔλθοις, ἢ τὸ πρὶν ἐν βίῳ·
καὶ γὰρ Ζεὺς ὅ, τι νεύσῃ
ξύν σοι τοῦτο τελευτᾷ.
καὶ τὸν ἐν Χαλύβεσσι
δαμάζει σὺν βίᾳ σίδαρον,
οὐδέ τις ἀποτόμου
λήματος ἐστὶν αἰδώς.

Στροφὴ β'.
καὶ σ᾽ ἐν ἀφύκτοισι χερῶν
εἷλε θεὰ δεσμοῖς.

ALCESTIS.

Pennis volavi per liquidum æthera
Scientiarum deliciis vacans,
   Suavesque tentavi recessus
      Pieridum vitreosque fontes;
Sed cuncta vincit dura Necessitas,
Quocunque vertor, non superabilis;
   Non ipse commisit tabellis
      Threiciis medicamen Orpheus;
Non Æsculapi toxica filiis
Phœbus, salutis pocula, miscuit;
   Quæ jura et obscœni valerent
      Imperium violare Fati.
Illa et Dearum sola tepentibus
Invidit aris; illa vel hostias
   Spernit reluctantes, et odit
      Marmoreæ simulacra formæ.
O Diva,—nam tu concilias Jovem
Et sceptra mundi—da placidam mihi
   Transire vitam: tu metalli
      Duritiem Chalybumque frangis
Immane ferrum; nec pudet indolem
Fovisse torvam.—Quo fugies, miser
   Admete? te fatale Numen
      Retibus implicuit dolosis!

τόλμα δ'· οὐ γὰρ ἀνά-
ξεις ποτ' ἔνερθεν
κλαίων τοὺς φθιμένους ἄνω.
καὶ θεῶν σκότιοι φθίνουσι
παῖδες ἐν θανάτῳ.
φίλα μὲν, ὅτ' ἦν μεθ' ἡμῶν,
φίλα δ' ἔτι καὶ θανοῦσα·
γενναιοτάταν δὲ πασᾶν
ἐζεύξω κλισίαις ἄκοιτιν.

'Αντ. β'.

μηδὲ νεκρῶν ὡς φθιμένων
χῶμα νομιζέσθω
τύμβος σᾶς ἀλόχου·
θεοῖσι δ' ὁμοίως
τιμάσθω σέβας ἐμπόρων.
καί τις δοχμίαν κέλευθον
ἐκβαίνων, τόδ' ἐρεῖ·
αὐτὰ ποτὲ προὔθανεν ἀνδρὸς,
νῦν δ' ἐστὶ μάκαιρα δαίμων.
χαῖρ', ὦ πότνι', εὖ δὲ δοίης.
τοῖαί νιν προσεροῦσι φᾶμαι.

EURIPIDES.

HOW D'YE DO?

ONE misty moisty morning,
    When cloudy was the weather,
There I met an old man
    Clothed all in leather,
With cap under his chin:
How d'ye do? and how d'ye do? and how d'ye do again?

GAMMER GURTON.

Sed ne queraris : nam neque lenient
Plutona fletus illacrymabilem ;
   Et ipsa descendit sub umbras
    Cimmerias soboles Deorum.
Quæ grata nostris vixit amoribus,
Illa in lacerto mortis amatior,
   Virtutis exemplar pudicæ
    Conjugibus socioque lecto.
Quin illa fœdi cespitis immemor
Errabit inter cœlicolum domos,
   Nigrisque mutabit cupressis
    Elysiæ juga læta sylvæ ;
Dicentque voces prætereuntium
Fauces sepulcri—' Sideribus vale
   Adscripta, pro caro libenter
    Ausa mori mulier marito !'

                              H. D.

QUOMODO TU VALEAS.

MANE vagans inter nebulas et flumina roris,
  Cum pluvio nubes incubuere polo,
Cuidam occurrebam domito senioribus annis,
  Ille senex corio totus amictus erat,
Pileolo mentum substrictus. Sæpe rogabam,
  ' Quomodo tu valeas ? quomodo tu valeas ?'
Atque iterum atque iterum mussabat uterque rogando,
  ' Quomodo tu valeas ? quomodo tu valeas ?'

                              F. H.

ON THE SPRING.

Lo ! where the rosy-bosomed hours
    Fair Venus' train appear,
Disclose the long-expecting flowers
    And wake the purple year !
The attic warbler pours her throat
Responsive to the cuckoo's note,
    The untaught harmony of spring :
While, whispering pleasure as they fly,
Cool Zephyrs through the clear blue sky
    Their gathered fragrance fling.

Where'er the oak's thick branches stretch
    A broader browner shade ;
Where'er the rude and moss-grown beech
    O'er-canopies the glade ;
Beside some water's rushy brink
With me the Muse shall sit, and think
    (At ease reclined in rustic state)
How vain the ardour of the crowd,
How low, how little are the proud,
    How indigent the great !

Still is the toiling hand of Care :
    The panting herds repose :
Yet hark, how through the peopled air
    The busy murmur glows !

IN VER.

CONVENIUNT roseis suffusæ risibus Horæ,
  Veris honos, Paphiæ gratia prima Deæ.
Protinus exsurgit brumali Flora cubili ;
  Nec mora, purpureas explicat annus opes.
Atthis et alterna respondens voce cucullus
  Indoctis iterant carmina verna modis ;
Dum festo interea reparans sua gaudia flatu,
  Cœruleum Zephyrus mulcet odore polum.

Quercus ubi radios obscuris frondibus arcet,
  Latior et saltus, densior umbra, subest ;
Frigida qua pinus, muscoque recondita fagus,
  Suppositæ nectunt pensile tegmen humo ;
Sit mihi, dum luxus atque otia rustica carpo,
  Et jaceo ad ripas dulce morantis aquæ,
Sit mihi cum Musa vulgi spectare tumultus,
  Qualia cum quanto vota furore petat ;
Quam vacuo tumeat vesana Superbia fastu ;
  Quæ sit in egregia nobilitate fames !

Rusticus excepit posito sudore quietem,
  Otia per campos fessa juvenca petit :
Audin', queis turbis glomerata frequentibus aura
  Ferveat, assiduis vivida facta sonis ?

The insect youth are on the wing,
Eager to taste the honied spring,
   And float amid the liquid noon:
Some lightly o'er the current skim,
Some shew their gaily-gilded trim
   Quick glancing to the sun.

To Contemplation's sober eye
   Such is the race of man:
And they that creep, and they that fly,
   Shall end where they began.
Alike the busy and the gay
But flutter through life's little day,
   In fortune's varying colours drest:
Brushed by the hand of rough Mischance,
Or chilled by age, their airy dance
   They leave, in dust to rest.

Methinks I hear in accents low
   The sportive kind reply—
Poor moralist! and what art thou?
   A solitary fly!
Thy joys no glittering female meets,
No hive hast thou of hoarded sweets,
   No painted plumage to display:
On hasty wings thy youth is flown;
Thy sun is set, thy spring is gone—
   We frolic while 'tis May.

GRAY.

Dædala funduntur flores examina circum,
  Lætaque melliferam depopulantur humum;
Aliger hic miles liquido fluitare sub æstu,
  Ille amat in summa ludere fontis aqua;
Atque alius, volitans super æthera præpete cursu,
  Corporis ostendit versicoloris opes.

Qui bene composita spectat mortalia mente,
  Sub paribus sentit legibus esse viros:
Qui cohibent gressus et qui velocius urgent,
  Ad metam, modo quam deseruere, volant.
Sorte nitent varia, fato sternuntur eodem,
  Qui sequitur vitæ gaudia, quique fugit;
Quocunque ereptus casu, sub pulvere dormit
  Pulvis, et aerii conticuere chori.

Forte aliquis cui cura joci, cui ludere cordi est,
  ‘Quid melius, tantum qui sapis’, inquit, ‘habes?’
Solus es, et nulla est cui jungas oscula conjux;
  Nulla domus, liquidas quæ tibi condat opes.
Non tua per cœlum pictos fert ala colores,
  Maturus periit flos tuus ante diem:
Sol tibi discessit; cecidit tibi gloria veris—
  Nos sequimur nostros, dum sinit hora, jocos.

W. G. H.

PROGRESS OF ADVICE.

SAYS Richard to Thomas—and seemed half afraid—
' I'm thinking to marry my mistress's maid.
Now because Mrs Lucy to thee is well known,
I'll do't if thou bid'st me or let it alone.
Now don't make a jest on't ; 'tis no jest to me,
In faith I'm in earnest, so prithee be free.
I have no fault to find with the girl since I knew her,
But I'd have thy advice e'er I tie myself to her.'
  Says Thomas to Richard—' to speak my opinion,
There's not such a brute in king George's dominion;
And I firmly believe, if you knew her as I do,
Thou would'st choose out a whipping post first to be
    tied to.
She's peevish, she's thievish, she's ugly, she's old,
And a liar and a fool and a slut and a scold.'
  Next day Richard hastened to Church and was wed,
And at night had informed her all Thomas had said.

SHENSTONE.

LITTLE BOY BLUET.

LITTLE boy Bluet, come blow me your horn,
The cow's in the meadow, the sheep in the corn :
But where is the little boy tending his sheep?
He's under the hay-cock fast asleep.

GAMMER GURTON.

UTERE CONSILIO.

'Mi Thoma,' Ricardus ait, simul anxius oris,
'Ancillam venit in mentem mihi ducere herilem.
Quando igitur tam nota tibi sit Lucia, si tu
Suaseris, hoc faciam; si non, rem prorsus omittam.
Parce cachinnari; nequeo indulgere cachinnis,
Seria ago: quare dic libera verba, sodalis.
Nullam, ex quo novi, detexi in virgine culpam:
Ante tamen vellem, quam res sit facta, moneri.'
   Cui Thomas male salsus—'ut omnia vera recludam,
Nulla est in toto tam bruta et sordida regno
Femina; quin credo, si tu modo tam bene noras,
Lictoris cædi virgis, quam ducere, malles.
Aspera, fur eadem, deformis, pejor ob annos,
Mendax, immunda, et stolida est, et cognita rixis.'
   Postera lux oritur: Ricardus ducit amatam;
Et monitus Thomæ sub nocte edixerat omnes!

                        B.

CŒRULE PARVE PUER.

Cœrule parve puer, cornu mihi fortiter infles:
   Vacca premit segetes, prata pererrat ovis:
Pro pudor! hic modus est quo, pastor, ovilia curas,
   Sub fœno domitus membra sopore gravi?

                        F. H.

PITT.

AND thou, blest star of Europe's darkest hour,
Whose words were wisdom, and whose counsels power,
Whom earth applauded through her peopled shores ;
Alas ! whom earth too early lost deplores :
Young without follies, without rashness bold,
And greatly poor amidst a nation's gold ;
In every veering gale of faction true,
Untarnished Chatham's genuine child, adieu !
Unlike our common suns, whose gradual ray
Expands from twilight to intenser day,
Thy blaze broke forth at once in full meridian sway.
O proved in danger ! not the fiercest flame
Of discord's rage thy constant soul could tame ;
Not when, far-striding o'er thy palsied land,
Gigantic treason took his bolder stand ;
Not when wild zeal, by murderous faction led,
On Wicklow's hills her grass-green banner spread ;
Or those stern conquerors of the restless wave
Defied the native soil they wont to save.—
Undaunted Patriot ! in that dreadful hour,
When pride and genius own a stronger power ;
When the dimmed eyeball and the struggling breath,
And pain and terror mark advancing death ;

PATER PATRIÆ.

Unica crescentes Europæ stella tenebras
  Dispulit, et brevis est gentibus orta salus :
O si nunc illo poteretur lumine tellus!
  Heu! demptum longis luctibus orba gemit.
Consiliis vires inerant, sapientia linguæ :
  Nulla foris metuit, nulla pericla domi.
Fortis nil temere est, juvenis nil ausus inepte :
  Et pauper patrias audiit inter opes.
O rerum variis, invicte, infesse, procellis ;
  Illustri soboles digna parente, vale!
Fulsisti, non ceu qui tarda crepuscula linquens
  Paulatim educit clarius usque jubar :
Extulit en subito tua se, et mortalibus ægris
  Integra maturo profuit igne dies.
Adfuit in quovis animus discrimine ; vel cum
  Seditio rabidum tolleret atra caput ;
Seu conjurati in campis viridantis Iernes
  Civili gererent impia bella manu ;
Sive ille, Oceani domitor, queis sueverat hostem
  Opprimere, in patrios verteret arma duces.
Illa etiam, quæ certa supervenit omnibus hora,
  Gloria cui demum cedit et ingenium ;
Qua victum cruciat dolor et metus ille futuri ;
  Torpet cæca acies ; pectora anhela tremunt ;

Still in that breast thy country held her throne,
Thy toil, thy fear, thy prayer were her's alone,
Thy last faint effort her's, and her's thy parting groan.

HEBER.

THE PIRATE'S FAREWELL.

FAREWELL! farewell!—the voice you hear
  Has left its last soft tone with you;
Its next must join the seaward cheer
  And shout among the shouting crew.

The accents, which I scarce could form
  Beneath your frown's controlling check,
Must give the word, above the storm,
  To cut the mast and clear the wreck.

The timid eye I dared not raise,
  The hand that shook when pressed to thine,
Must point the guns upon the chase,
  Must bid the deadly cutlass shine.

To all I love or hope or fear,
  Honour or own—a long adieu!
To all that life has soft and dear,
  Farewell—save memory of you!

SCOTT.

Illa, quæ tua sunt vix huc memor usque malorum,
  Pro patria sanctas fundis, ut ante, preces :
Una tibi curæ vivo fuit, una sub ipso
  Funere : suprema ' Patria' voce gemis.

W. J. L.

PIRATÆ VALEDICTIO.

Vale ! supremam nostra vox dulcedinem
  Tecum reliquit—ah ! vale,
Dilecta virgo ! Nunc strepente nautico
  Clamore primus audiar.
Qui proferebam blanda vix suspiria
  Vultu pavescens sub tuo,
Malum recidi turbidos inter notos,
  Quassamque purgari ratem,
Clarus jubebo. Qui levare conscia
  Non ausus in te lumina,
Qui tam tremiscens contigi manum tuam,
  Belli excitatus impetu,
Tormenta in hostes dirigam sequacia,
  Gladiumque tollam fulgidum.
Quæcunque amoris dona, gloriæ, spei
  Fuistis infausto mihi,
Valete, longum—semper at tui memor
  Manebit hic miserrimus.

F. H.

THE PIG AND THE PIPER'S SON.

Tom, Tom, the piper's son,
Stole a pig, and away he run:
The pig was eat, and Tom was beat,
And Tom ran crying down the street.

GAMMER GURTON.

MY NATIVE VALE.

Dear is my little native vale,
  The ringdove builds and murmurs there,
Close to my cot she tells her tale
  To every passing villager;
The squirrel leaps from tree to tree,
And shells his nuts at liberty.

Through orange groves and myrtle bowers
  That breathe a gale of fragance round,
I charm the fairy-footed hours
  With the loved lute's romantic sound;
Or crowns of living laurel weave,
For those that win the race at eve.

The Shepherd's horn at break of day,
  The ballet danced in twilight shade;
The canzonet and roundelay
  Sung in the silent greenwood glade,
These simple joys that never fail
Shall bind me to my native vale.

ROGERS.

PORCUS ET CITHARISTÆ FILIUS.

ILLE citharistæ filius,
Thomas, Thomas nominatus,
Porculo surrepto currit:
Porcus cito manducatus,
Thomas, cito verberatus,
Ululans per vicum fur it,
Ululans per vicum fur it.

F. H.

VALLIS NATALIS.

VALLIS amo latebras et parvula rura paternæ,
  Qua gemit in viridi blanda columba domo,
Qua mollem assidui fabellam narrat amoris,
  Pagano nostram prætereunte casam :
Mus saliens omni silvester ab arbore pendet,
  Lætasque impavido pascitur ore nuces.

Hic citreos inter fructus myrtique sub umbra,
  Plenus ubi a patulis floribus halat odor,
Fallimus alipedes positi feliciter horas
  Suaviloquæ sonitu nobiliore lyræ ;
Seu placeat vivas magis internectere lauros,
  Si quis Olympiacum vespere currat iter.

Sub matutinum pastoris buccina solem,
  Saltibus impliciti, sole cadente, pedes ;
Quodque lyræ canitur, vel quos modulatur arundo,
  Inter Hamadryadum frondea rura, choros ;
Simplicis hæc durant casta oblectamina vitæ,
  Et teneor magno vallis amore meæ.

H. D.

THE LOTOS EATERS.

How sweet it were, hearing the downward stream,
With half-shut eyes ever to seem
Falling asleep in a half-dream!
To dream and dream, like yonder amber light,
Which will not leave the myrrh bush on the height;
To hear each other's whispered speech;
Eating the lotos, day by day,
To watch the crisping ripples on the beach,
And tender curving lines of creamy spray:
To lend our hearts and spirits wholly
To the influence of mild-minded melancholy;
To muse and brood and live again in memory,
With the old faces of our infancy
Heaped over with a mound of grass,
Two handfuls of white dust shut in an urn of brass.

TENNYSON.

TO MARKET.

To market, to market, to buy a plum bun;
Home again, home again, market is done.

GAMMER GURTON.

LOTOPHAGI.

Ut lentis juvat imminere somnis,
Et proni sonitum tenere rivi,
Dum marcent oculi, diesque fessis
Intermortua palpebris hebescit :
Inque oblivia grata diffluentes,
Vixdum, ceu jubar aureum, morari,
Quod summis nemorum comis adhærens
Sistit languidulo nitore noctem!
Haurire ut comitum leves susurros ;
Loton carpere, prandiis vacare :
Ut fluctus maris interosculantes
Spectare, et teneros cientis orbes
Spumæ lacteolos sequi meatus!
His nec Mœstitiæ placens imago
Dulcem desinat implicare fraudem :
Sic fas sit sine fine somniare ;
Sic in condita temporum relabi,
Dum visæ veteres subesse formæ,
Quas infantia noverit, Penatum ;
Et suetæ species et ora nostrum,
Quæ cespes premit et recondit urna
Selibra cineris coacta cani.

C. M.

AD NUNDINAS.

Vade forum, tu vade forum, confectaque prunis
Liba eme ; res illic acta ; recurre domum.

F. H.

HARP OF THE NORTH.

HARP of the North, farewell! The hills grow dark,
  On purple peaks a deeper shade descending;
In twilight copse the glow-worm lights her spark;
  The deer half-seen are to the covert wending.
Resume thy wizard elm! the fountain lending,
  And the wild breeze, thy wilder minstrelsy;
Thy numbers sweet with nature's vespers blending,
  With distant echo from the fold and lea,
And herdboy's evening pipe and hum of housing bee.

Yet once again farewell, thou minstrel Harp!
  Yet once again forgive my feeble sway;
And little reck I of the censure sharp
  May idly cavil at an idle lay.
Much have I owed thy strains on life's long way,
  Through secret woes the world has never known,
When on the weary night dawned wearier day,
  And bitterer was the grief devoured alone.
That I o'erlive such woes, Enchantress, is thine own!

                                        SCOTT.

CITHARA CALEDONIÆ.

Orta Caledoniis valeas, Cithara, orta sub antris!
    Purpureis major montibus umbra cadit:
Emicat in saltu seræ lampyridos ignis,
    Cerva petit tectum vix bene visa nemus.
Tu magicam repetas ulmum; fontique ministres,
    Et rudibus ventis, quæ rudiora sonas;
Dum tibi respondet pleni concentus ovilis,
    Et pecudum a longo vox repetita jugo;
Nec vespertini cessat pastoris arundo,
    Nec prima reducum nocte susurrus apum.

Ergo iterum valeas, Cithara, acceptissima vati!
    De nostris habeas crimina nulla modis:
Non horrere meum est linguam censoris acuti,
    Si qua levi dicto vox leve vellat opus.
Multa tuis modulis, per longæ tædia vitæ,
    Debuit arcanis mens mea pressa malis;
Cum pepulit noctis tristes lux tristior umbras,
    Curaque erat gravior, quam sine teste tuli.
Quod mihi per tantos suffecit vita labores,
    Quod spiro et valeo, muneris omne tui est.

                            B. H. D.

MOLOCH.

My sentence is for open war: of wiles
More unexpert I boast not; them let those
Contrive who need, or when they need, not now.
For while they sit contriving, shall the rest,
Millions that stand in arms and longing wait
The signal to ascend, sit lingering here
Heaven's fugitives, and for their dwelling-place
Accept this dark opprobrious den of shame,
The prison of his tyranny, who reigns
By our delay?   No, let us rather choose,
Armed with hell flames and fury, all at once,
O'er heaven's high towers to force resistless way,
Turning our tortures into horrid arms
Against the torturer; when to meet the noise
Of his almighty engine he shall hear
Infernal thunder, and for lightning, see
Black fire and horror shot with equal rage
Among his angels, and his throne itself
Mixed with Tartarean sulphur, and strange fire,
His own invented torments.

MILTON.

MOLOCH LOQUITUR.

BELLA placent nobis: nobis ars unica bellum,
Nec plures didicisse volo: quibus utile, cæcas
Consilii ambages jactent artemque sequentur.
Non hoc ista sibi tempus molimina poscit;
Nam dum quisque dolos texit vafer atque retexit,
En! cœlo profugæ stant circum mille cohortes,
Armatisque fremunt dextris, et signa reposcunt
Expectata diu, si quando limina cœli
Aspiciant: nostri interea nigrantia lustra
Sedibus optatis fœdique opprobria mutant
Carceris, atque alii tradunt sua regna morando.
Quin potius flammis Erebi cæcoque furore
Armati simul irruimus, cursuque per auras
Præcipiti summas cœli superavimus arces,
Torquentes nova tela manu tormentaque ab ipso
Addita, et in cœlum cœli convertimus iras.
Audiet ille suum ad fulmen reboantia regna
Inferno tonitru, nec nostræ fulgura turmæ
Defuerint; tanto fremitu furor evomet atros
Inter cœlicolas ignes, soliumque replebit
Sulfure Tartareo et piceæ caligine nubis,
Effundetque novas flammas, inventa tyranni.

G. C.

THE DILEMMA.

If all the world were apple pie,
  And all the sea were ink,
And all the trees were bread and cheese,
  My stars! what should we drink?

Gammer Gurton.

THE BURIAL OF SIR JOHN MOORE.

Not a sound was heard, not a funeral note,
  As his corse to the ramparts we hurried;
Not a soldier discharged his farewell shot,
  O'er the grave where our hero we buried.

We buried him deep at dead of night,
  The sod with our bayonets turning,
By the struggling moonbeam's misty light,
  And the lanthorn dimly burning.

No useless coffin enclosed his breast,
  Nor in sheet or shroud we wound him,
But he lay like a warrior taking his rest
  With his martial cloak around him.

Few and short were the prayers we said,
  And we spoke not a word of sorrow;
But we stedfastly gazed on the face of the dead,
  And we bitterly thought of the morrow.

We thought as we hollowed his narrow bed,
  And smoothed down his lonely pillow,
That the foe and the stranger would tread o'er his head,
  And we far away on the billow!

VEXATA QUÆSTIO.

Sɪ Terra e pistis constaret inhospita pomis,
Si foret Oceanus vasti lacus atramenti,
Si folia in silvis panisque et caseus essent—
Pro facinus! per ego hos oculos, per sidera testor,
Nescio quid biberent sitientia sæcla virorum!

H. D.

DUCIS EXSEQUIÆ.

Bᴜᴄᴄɪɴᴀ nulla dedit, nec tristem nænia vocem,
    In vallum tulimus nos ubi membra Ducis;
Non solito miles decoravit honore sepulcrum,
    Martia non solitos arma dedere sonos.

Undique constabant horrenda silentia noctis,
    Luna laborantes vix agitabat equos;
Lumina præbebant incerto lampades igne,
    Hasta sepulcralem dura cavabat humum.

Nulla cedrus legit cineres nec inutilis urna,
    Nec sunt funerea pectora amicta toga:
Ac veluti in castris miles dat membra quieti,
    Implicitus proprio sic erat ille sago.

Tam brevibus super exsequiis non multa precamur,
    Nec vox est luctum testificata gravem;
Dumque recensemus mala quæ lux crastina ferret,
    In vultu occisi figimus ora ducis.

Et gladiis vilem dum sic exsculpsimus arcam,
    Stravimus et solum, cura suprema, torum;
Glebam insultabunt hostes, reputamus, in illam,
    Dum sequimur reduci nos freta longa via.

Lightly they'll talk of the spirit that's gone,
  And o'er his cold ashes upbraid him;
But little he'll reck, if they'll let him sleep on,
  In the grave where a Briton has laid him.

But half of our dreary task was done,
  When the clock told the hour of retiring;
And we heard the distant and random gun,
  That the foe was sullenly firing.

Slowly and sadly we laid him down
  From the field of his fame fresh and gory;
We carved not a line, we raised not a stone,
  But we left him alone in his glory.

WOLFE.

HEY MY CHICKEN.

Hey my chicken, my chicken,
  And hey my chicken, my deary!
Such a sweet pet as this
  Was neither far nor neary.

Here we go up up up,
  And here we go down down downy,
And here we go backwards and forwards,
  And here we go round round roundy!

GAMMER GURTON.

Compositi tantos leviter censebit honores
   Quilibet, atque ipsum per gelida ossa virum ;
Nil illi curæ, placida modo dormiat herba,
   Britones extremo quam posuere solo.

Nec media invisi pars est exacta laboris,
   Noctis ut admonitu prægravis hora sonat :
Quin proludentem ad pugnas audivimus hostem,
   Et pigra fulmineas fert temere aura minas.

Vulneribusque novis et honesto sanguine fusum,
   Paulatim dedimus triste cadaver humo ;
Nec struimus cippum nec sculptum in marmore nomen :
   Deserto superest Gloria sola Duci.

J. H.

O MEA PULLULA.

O MEA pullula blandula,
   O mea pullula suavis,
Procul in terris aut prope
   Non est, ut hæc, rara avis!

Hic en! ascendimus cœlos,
   Et hic ubi locus est imus ;
Hic rursum et prorsum cursamur,
   Et circum et circum redimus.

F. H.

MARY.

MARY, I believed thee true,
    And I was blest in thus believing;
But now I mourn that e'er I knew
    A girl so fair and so deceiving.
Few have ever loved like me—
    Yes, I have loved thee too sincerely!
And few have e'er deceived like thee:
    Alas, deceived me too severely!

Fare thee well!—yet think awhile
    On one whose bosom bleeds to doubt thee;
Who now would rather trust that smile,
    And die with thee, than live without thee.
Fare thee well!—I'll think of thee:
    Thou leav'st me many a bitter token;
For see, distracting woman, see—
    My peace is gone, my heart is broken!

                                        MOORE.

DELIA FALSA.

DELIA, credideram tu saltem fida fuisses;
    Et spe quam dederas tu mihi lætus eram:
Sed modo tam pulcram queror invenisse puellam
    Fallere, perjuris in mea damna labris.
Non face plebeia, solitis non ignibus uror:
    Heu! nimio fueram captus amore tui.
Nec mea plebeiam texisti in pectora fraudem,
    Perfida!—quam vere perfida dicta mihi!

Delia falsa, vale!—sed adhuc reminiscere nostri;
    Est, nequit acceptam qui dubitare fidem;
Qui risu pendere tuo, qui nunc quoque mallet
    Tecum, quam sine te vivere, posse mori.
Delia falsa, vale!—tua sæpe recurret imago,
    Tot memori linquis tristia signa proco;
Inspice enim hoc miserum pectus, sævissima rerum!
    Inspice—tu leti causa ferere mei.

                  H. D.

Restat, ut ascribat litera nostra

VALE.

PARS SECUNDA.

     With awe I kneel
Trembling before the footstool of thy state,
My God, my Father!—I will sing to thee
A hymn of laud, a solemn canticle,
Ere on the cypress wreath, which overshades
The throne of Death, I hang my mournful lyre,
And give its wild strings to the desert gale.

ἀπάντων τῶν ἐπὶ τῆς γῆς τέλος ἐστὶν

Ὁ ΘΕΟΣ.

TO THE READER.

THAT union of the soul and body here,
Which heaven has ordered, calls for several treatment
To suit its several parts—Our outward man
Asks cheerful exercise ; our inward man
Must have his pauses too from serious thought,
And gathers vigour for his loftier flights
By earthly relaxation—Yet, my friend,
We must not hover here, nor skim the turf
Uninterruptedly, but imp our wings
For rocks aerial and for upper day.

AD LECTOREM.

Terrena mentis corporisque vincula,
Deo jubente fabricata, diligunt
Poscuntque curas hinc et inde compares.
Corpus quiete roboratur utili,
Modicisque gaudet indies laboribus.
Mens otiosa crescit interim mora,
Vigetque, nil molita. Sed, dulcissime,
Non hic moremur; neu solum diutius
Penna supervolemus ignava nimis:
Sed altiores audeamus ætheris
Tranare campos, et die puro frui.

LITANY TO THE HOLY SPIRIT.

In the hour of my distress,
When temptations sore oppress,
And when I my sins confess—
    Sweet Spirit, comfort me!

When I lie within my bed,
Sick in heart and sick in head,
And with doubts discomfited—
    Sweet Spirit, comfort me!

When the house doth sigh and weep,
And the world is drowned in sleep,
Yet mine eyes their vigils keep—
    Sweet Spirit, comfort me!

When the passing bell doth toll,
And the furies in a shoal
Come to fright my parting soul—
    Sweet Spirit, comfort me!

When the tapers all burn blue,
When the comforters are few,
And that number more than true,—
    Sweet Spirit, comfort me!

When the priest his last has prayed,
And I nod to what is said,
'Cause my speech is now decayed—
    Sweet Spirit, comfort me!

AD SANCTUM SPIRITUM.

HORA in calamitatis,
Cum tenter et prober satis,
O! ut solvar a peccatis,
    Solare, dulcis Spiritus!

Cum capite et corde æger
Miser intus lecto tegar,
Ne in tenebras releger,
    Solare, dulcis Spiritus!

Quando domus flet et gemit,
Atque sopor mundum premit,
Nec vigiliis me demit,
    Solare, dulcis Spiritus!

Quum campana sonat mortem,
Furiæque vim consortem
Jungunt, rapiant ut fortem,
    Solare, dulcis Spiritus!

Lampas fuscos dat colores;
Pauci adstant, qui dolores
Levent—veri pauciores!
    Solare, dulcis Spiritus!

Cum sacerdos summa dabit
Verba, quæ nutu probabit
Caput hoc, si vox negabit,
    Solare, dulcis Spiritus!

When (God knows) I'm tossed about
Either with despair or doubt;
Yet before the glass runs out—
       Sweet Spirit, comfort me!

When the tempter me pursueth
With the sins of all my youth,
And half damns me with their truth—
       Sweet Spirit, comfort me!

When the flames and hellish cries
Fright my ears and fright my eyes,
And all terrors me surprise—
       Sweet Spirit, comfort me!

When the judgment is revealed,
And that open, which was sealed,
When to thee I have appealed—
       Sweet Spirit, comfort me!
              HERRICK.

PSALM XIX.

THE spacious firmament on high,
And all the blue etherial sky,
The spangled heavens, a shining frame,
Their great original proclaim.

Cum huc illuc (Deus novit)
Ferar, sicut terror movit,
Nec stat sanguis, qui me fovit,
    Solare, dulcis Spiritus!

Cum peccatis me juventæ
Serpens premit violentæ,
Vero heu! consentiente,
    Solare, dulcis Spiritus!

Aures gemitus obtundunt!
Ignes oculos confundunt!
Nervi sine te succumbunt!
    Solare, dulcis Spiritus!

En! judicium declaratur:
En! patet quod celabatur:
En! vox iras deprecatur—
    Solare, dulcis Spiritus!
            H. D.

PSALMUS XIX.

Quicquid habet cœli vertex et splendidus ordo,
    Quicquid habent vasti cœrula templa poli,
Sidera quot splendent, quot sunt super æthera flammæ,
    Omnia divinum testificantur opus.

The unwearied sun from day to day
Does his Creator's praise display,
And publishes to every land
The work of an Almighty hand.

Soon as the evening shades prevail,
The moon takes up the wondrous tale,
And nightly to the listening earth
Repeats the story of her birth—

While all the stars that round her burn,
And all the planets in their turn,
Confirm the tidings as they roll,
And spread the truth from pole to pole.

What though in solemn silence all
Move round the dark terrestrial ball,
What though nor voice nor minstrel sound
Among their radiant orbs be found—

With saints and angels they rejoice,
And utter forth a glorious voice,
For ever singing as they shine,
"The hand that made us is divine."

ADDISON.

Sol qualis niteat, quali sit origine natus,
    Indicia, assiduo dum redit orbe, facit;
Per quascumque vagum late jubar extulit oras,
    Sedulus Artificem prædicat ille suum.

Quum modo victrices descendunt vesperis umbræ,
    Excipit alternam Luna diserta vicem;
Et sua miranti memorans primordia terræ,
    Edita quo fundat lumina fonte, refert.

Illius ætherium quot servant sidera cursum,
    Quot gyri in cœlo, noctivagæque faces,
Singula confirmant cantu, quæ singula narrant,
    Et capit unanimes axis uterque modos.

Ergone, terrestrem circa dum volvitur orbem,
    Stella secat tacitam pendula quæque viam?
Ergone Sol nullos, nullos dant astra susurros,
    Nec faciunt de tot millibus ulla sonum?

Scilicet angelicos interlabentia cætus
    Clarescunt superi murmura læta poli;
Et canere auditæ per tanta silentia voces:
    FINGIMUR ÆTERNA DIRIGIMURQUE MANU.

                       W. G. H.

PROPAGATION OF THE GOSPEL.

From Greenland's icy mountains,
    From India's coral strand,
Where Afric's sunny fountains
    Roll down their golden sand;
From many an ancient river,
    From many a palmy plain,
They call us to deliver
    Their land from error's chain.

What though the spicy breezes
    Blow soft o'er Java's isle,
Though every prospect pleases
    And only man is vile?
In vain with lavish kindness
    The gifts of God are strewn,
The heathen in his blindness
    Bows down to wood and stone.

Can we, whose souls are lighted
    With wisdom from on high,
Can we to men benighted,
    The lamp of life deny?
Salvation! oh—Salvation!
    The joyful sound proclaim;
Till each remotest nation
    Has learnt Messiah's name!

ITE IN OMNES TERRAS.

THULES ab usque montibus
Albo gelu rigentibus;
Ab India, qua curali
Vincunt arenas aggeres;
Aurumque qua devolvitur
Afri ex apricis amnibus;
Multo e vetusto flumine,
Multisque palmetis simul,
" Adeste," clamant " tollite
Erroris atra vincula !"

Quid thure si, si balsamo
Odora Javæ litora,
Si rura pulcriora sunt,
Homoque solus vilis est?
Frustra Dei benignitas
Sic largiter dedit manu—
Caliginosus Ethnicus
Deos adorat ligneos !

Et nos, quibus veri sacrum
Effulsit e cœlo jubar,
Cæcis viris negabimus
Vitæ, viæque lampada?
Salutis O—Salutis O,
Enunciate gloriam,
Extrema donec litora
Sonant Iesu nomine !

Waft, waft, ye winds, his story,
   And you, ye waters, roll,
Till like a sea of glory
   It spreads from pole to pole :
Till o'er our ransomed nature,
   The Lamb for sinners slain,
Redeemer, King, Creator,
   In bliss returns to reign !

HEBER.

SONG OF SIMEON.

LORD, now lettest thou thy servant depart in peace,
For mine eyes have seen thy salvation,
Which thou hast prepared before the face of all people;
To be a light to lighten the Gentiles,
And to be the glory of thy people Israel.

ST LUKE ii. 29.

Quod fecit, et quod pertulit,
Auræ ferant, ferant aquæ,
Dum sempiterna Veritas
Utrumque pervadat polum ;
Dum purus Agnus, sanguine
Lotos revisurus suo,
Rector, Redemptor, Artifex
Descendat in terras Deus !

B.

CANIT SIMEON.

DOMINE, jam patiaris
Servum, quem tuum vocaris,
 In pace discedere ;

Cum tuæ jubar salutis
Viderim, ut institutis
 Docuisti credere :

Jubar, quod parasti coram
Oculis tu populorum
 Sæculis in omnibus ;

Jubar, quod illuminaret
Gentes, gloriamque daret
 Israel nepotibus.

H. D.

It is the man of God, who was disobedient unto the word of the Lord.
1 Kings xiii. 26.

PROPHET of God, arise and take
With thee the words of wrath divine,
 The scourge of heaven, to shake
 O'er yon apostate shrine.

Where angels down the lucid stair
Came hovering to our sainted sires,
 Now in the twilight glare
 The heathen's wizard fires.

Go, with thy voice the altar rend;
Scatter the ashes; be the arm,
 That idols would befriend,
 Shrunk at thy withering charm!

Then turn thee, for thy time is short,
But trace not o'er the former way,
 Lest idol pleasures court
 Thy heedless soul astray.

Thou know'st how hard to hurry by,
Where on the lonely woodland road
 Beneath the moonlight sky
 The festal warblings flowed;

Where maidens to the Queen of Heaven
Wove the gay dance round oak or palm,
 Or breathed their vows at even
 In hymns as soft as balm.

VATES SURGE DEI.

VATES surge Dei!—Surge, et adulteram
In gentem æthereas præcipita minas:
    Flagrum concute cœli
    Hoc fanum super impium!

Scalis agmen ubi pensile lucidis
Devenere pios Angelicum patres,
    Nunc falsæ magica aræ
    Splendet flamma crepusculo.

I, devota cadant saxa sub hostia!
I, sparge et cineres!—brachia macera
    Torva voce, profanas
    Amplectentia imagines.

Tum, nec longa mora est, verte retro pedes:
Calcanda est eadem non tibi semita,
    Ne qua impura voluptas
    Mentem fascinet insciam.

Scis quam difficile est prætereuntibus,
Qua solis placidorum in nemorum jugis
    Pulcræ sub face Lunæ
    Festum perstrepuit melos;

Qua palma aut viridi læta sub ilice
Dianam celebrant carmina virginum,
    Lascivæque choreæ et
    Vespertinus odor precum.

Or thee perchance a darker spell
Enthralls: the smooth stones of the flood,
　　By mountain grot or fell,
　　Pollute with infant's blood;

The giant altar on the rock,
The cavern whence the timbrel's call
　　Affrights the wandering flock :—
　　Thou long'st to search them all.

Trust not the dangerous path again—
O forward step and lingering will!
　　O loved and warned in vain!
　　And wilt thou perish still?

Thy message given, thine home in sight,
To the forbidden feast return?
　　Yield to the false delight
　　Thy better soul could spurn?

Alas, my brother! round thy tomb
In sorrow kneeling, and in fear,
　　We read the Pastor's doom,
　　Who speaks and will not hear.

The gray haired saint may fail at last,
The surest guide a wanderer prove;
　　Death only binds us fast
　　To the bright shore of love.

KEBLE.

Seu forte insidiæ te magis impiæ
Seducant—vitreus te lapis amnium,
    Hirto montis in antro aut
    Sparsis sanguine vallibus;

Altare in scopulis vastum adamantinis;
Spelunca, unde greges terruit avios
    Sistri mysticus horror—
    Ardes omnia quærere.

I calles alios: crede periculo—
O præceps gradus, O propositi mora!
    O frustra morieris
    Fati sic monitus tui?

Jussis rite datis, ante oculos domo,
Impermisse, dapes ad vetitas redis?
    Falso cedis amori,
    Quem spernes animosior?

Heu! dilecte, tuo in cespite supplices
Gravi tristitia sternimur et metu,
    Pastoremque dolemus,
    Qui fert jussa nec audiet.

Vates in senio sic cadit ultimo;
Fidens in media dux dubitat via!
    Sola morte ligamur
    Puræ litoribus Fide.

                  H. D.

GOOD FRIDAY.

Bound upon the accursed tree,
Faint and bleeding, who is He?
By the eyes so pale and dim,
Streaming blood and writhing limb,
By the flesh with scourges torn,
By the crown of twisted thorn,
By the sides so deeply pierced,
By the baffled burning thirst,
By the drooping death-dewed brow—
Son of Man! 'tis Thou! 'tis Thou!

Bound upon the accursed tree,
Dread and awful, who is He?
By the sun at noonday pale,
Shivering rocks and rending veil,
By earth that trembles at his doom,
By yonder saints who burst their tomb,
By Eden, promised e'er He died,
To the felon by his side,
Lord! our suppliant knees we bow—
Son of God! 'tis Thou! 'tis Thou!

DIES PASSIONIS.

ARBORE in funesta fixus,
Languens, cruentatus, Ille
Quis est?—pallidis ocellis,
Sanguine, et convulsis membris,
Carne flagris lacerata,
Capite intertexto spinis,
Latere intus penetrato,
Siti fervida, derisa,
Fronte letum prolocuta—
Te videmus, Te fatemur,
Hominis dolende Fili !

Arbore in funesta fixus,
Quis est obstupendus Ille ?
Meridiano sole nigro,
Rupibus quassatis, Templi
Velo penitus disrupto,
Trepidante circum terra
Teste tam tremendæ mortis;
Paradiso tum promisso
Exspiranti prope Furi—
Te videmus, Te fatemur,
Et te veneramur omnes,
Dei manifeste Fili !

Bound upon the accursed tree,
Sad and dying who is He?
By the last and bitter cry,
The ghost given up in agony;
By the lifeless body laid
In the chamber of the dead;
By the mourners come to weep,
Where the bones of Jesus sleep;
Crucified! we know Thee now;
Son of man! 'tis Thou! 'tis Thou!

Bound upon the accursed tree,
Dread and awful who is He?
By the prayer for them that slew—
"Lord they know not what they do"—
By the spoiled and empty grave,
By the souls He died to save,
By the conquest He hath won,
By the saints before his throne,
By the rain-bow round his brow—
Son of God! 'tis Thou! 'tis Thou!

MILMAN.

Arbore in funesta fixus,
Quis est moribundus Ille?
Ultima et lugubri voce ;
Spiritu exeunte diros
Inter mortis cruciatus ;
Corpore defuncto mœstis
Strato locis mortuorum ;
Accedentibus amicis,
Ut ad ossa Christi flerent—
Crucifixe !—Te fatemur,
Hominis dolende Fili !

Arbore in funesta fixus
Quis est obstupendus Ille?
Prece pro nefandis ipsis
Trucidantibus oblata—
' Pater nesciunt quid agant !'
Tumulo vacante, victo,
Animis per te redemptis,
Ineffabili triumpho,
Sine numero Beatis
Circa solium supremum
Deponentibus coronas,
Arcu irradiante frontem—
Te videmus, Te fatemur,
Dei manifeste Fili !

F. H.

MOUNT SAINT BERNARD.

WHERE these rude rocks on Bernard's summit nod,
    Once heavenwards sprung the throne of Pennine Jove,
    An ancient shrine of hospitable Love,
Now burns the altar to the Christian's God.
Here peaceful Piety, age on age, has trod
    The waste; still keeps her vigils, takes her rest;
    Still as of yore salutes the coming guest,
And cheers the weary as they onward rove,
Healing each wayworn limb—or oft will start
    Catching the storm-lost wanderer's sinking cry,
Speed the rich cordial to his ebbing heart,
    Chafe his stiff limbs and bid him not to die.
So tasked to smooth stern Winter's drifting wing,
And garb the eternal snows in more eternal spring.

                                Δ.

ALMS.

GIVE, if thou can'st an alms; if not, afford
Instead of that a sweet and gentle word;
God crowns our goodness, wheresoe'er He sees
On our part wanting the abilities.

                                HERRICK.

SCRIPTUM IN MONTE BERNARDI.

Hæc ubi saxa vides Bernardi in monte, viator,
    Pennini quondam templa fuere Jovis,
Hospitium vetus, et multis memorabile sæclis ;
    Nunc colitur veri sanctior ara Dei.
Scilicet hic olim voluit sibi ponere sedem
    Religio, et notis gaudet adesse jugis ;
Utque prius blanda venientes voce salutat,
    Deque via fessis alma ministrat opem,
Et fractas reparat vires, reficitque medela,
    Et fovet Alpino membra perusta gelu ;
Aut, quos obruerit subita nix lapsa ruina,
    Eripit ex alta mole, vetatque mori.
Temperat et Boreæ rabiem, mollitque pruinas,
    Et facit æterno vere tepere nives.

S. B.

LARGITIO.

Si nummos habeas, da quod habes ; si minus id vales,
Da solatiolum dulciloquis et teneris labris :
Si quid fecerimus corde pio, plaudit opus Pater,
Qui nos instituit rerum inopes, et miserans videt.

B.

BY THE WATERS OF BABYLON.

By the waters of Babylon we sat down and wept,

When we remembered thee, O Sion.

As for our harps we hanged them up

Upon the trees that are therein.

For they that led us away captive

Required of us then a song

And melody in our heaviness;

Sing us one of the songs of Sion.

How shall we sing the Lord's song in a strange land?

If I forget thee, O Jerusalem,

Let my right hand forget her cunning.

If I do not remember thee,

Let my tongue cleave to the roof of my mouth;

Yea, if I prefer not Jerusalem in my mirth.

Remember the children of Edom, O Lord,

In the day of Jerusalem: how they said,

Down with it, down with it, even to the ground.

PROPTER AMNES BABYLONIS.

PROPTER amnes Babylonis
Sedebamus lacrymantes,
Templi sancti et Sionis
Triste fatum complorantes ;

Et ad salices propinquas,
Conspergentes ora fletu,
Fractas figebamus lyras
Plurimo cum ejulatu :

Namque amabilem concentum
Exquirebant vexatores,
Jubilemus ut recentum
Inter cladium dolores ;

Et clamabant, " Delectentur
Hostes versibus divinis !"
Quomodo Dei cantentur
Carmina in peregrinis ?

Dextra moveri negato,
Si Sionis obliviscar ;
Lingua hæreat palato,
Templi si non reminiscar.

Pende exultationem,
Deus, Arabum, et minas
Quas fuderunt, ut Sionem
Convertebant in ruinas,

O daughter of Babylon, wasted with misery,
Yea, happy shall he be that rewardeth thee
As thou hast served us.
Blessed shall he be that taketh thy children,
And throweth them against the stones.

PSALM CXXXVII.

HOME.

BANISHED the house of sacred rest,
  Amid a thoughtless throng,
At length I heard its creed confessed,
  And knelt the saints among.

Artless his strain and unadorned,
  Who spoke Christ's message there;
But what at home I might have scorned,
  Now charmed my famished ear.

Lord, grant me this abiding grace,
  Thy words and sons to know;
To pierce the veil on Moses' face,
  Although his speech be slow.

LYRA APOSTOLICA.

Ut fremebant " Devastate
Solymorum ornamenta,
Et cum solo adæquate
Urbis alta fundamenta."

Felix erit, Babylonis
Nata, curis jam vexata,
In te die ultionis
Qui rependet nostra fata.

Felix erit, qui infantes
Cum parentibus excidet,
Et ad lapides extantes
Vitam fragilem elidet.

A. B. H.

DOMUS.

Sacræ quietis exul a pura domo,
    Inter sodales improbos,
Tandem audii perculsus expostam fidem,
    Addorque sanctorum gregi.

Auctor modestæ castus eloquentiæ
    Fuit ille Christi nuncius :
Sed nunc, quod ante spreveram surdus domi,
    Auri irruit famelicæ.

O sempiterna gratia sinas mihi
    Te scire, Deus, et tuos :
Velata Mosis ora acutum cernere,
    Sermone sit quamvis rudi !

H. D.

TO DEATH.

Thou bidst me come away,
And I'll no longer stay,
Than for to shed some tears
For faults of former years,
And to repent some crimes
Done in the present times ;
To don my robes of love
Fit for the place above ;
To gird my loins about
With charity throughout :
And so to travel hence
With feet of innocence.
This done, I'll only cry
" God mercy !"—and so die.

Herrick.

EPITAPH.

Beneath a sleeping infant lies—
  To earth his body lent,
Hereafter shall more glorious rise,
  But not more innocent.
And when the arch-angel's trump shall blow,
  And souls to bodies join,
Thousands will wish their lives below,
  Had been as short as thine.

Wisbeach Churchyard.

AD MORTEM.

Jubes abire, nec recuso,
Lacrymarum rore fuso,
Culpis pro præteritorum
Juvenilium annorum,
Et, in corde pœnitenti,
Tempore pro hoc præsenti.
Quin et pallium amoris
Induam, quo pergam foris,
Quod velare me sit aptum
Inter cœlites correptum.
Sic succinctæ pietate,
Innocentia ligatæ,
Iter plantæ inchoabunt ;
Et suprema exclamabunt
" Miserere pecatoris,
Deus !" verba hujus oris.

H. D.

M. S.

Parvulus hic infans molli sub cespite dormit,
    Credita sunt viridi, non data, membra solo ;
Pulcrior exuta posthac tellure resurget,
    Tempore sed nullo castior esse potest.
Quum tamen attonitos rumpet Tuba nuntia cœlos,
    Junctaque sint animis ossa relicta suis,
Mille tuo optabunt vitam degisse sub astro,
    Inque brevi tecum deperiisse die.

H. I. H.

THY WILL BE DONE.

My God, my Father, while I stray
Far from my home in life's rough way,
O teach me from my heart to say,
　　　　　Thy will be done!

Though dark my fate and sad my lot,
Let me be still and murmur not;
But breathe the prayer divinely taught—
　　　　　Thy will be done!

What though in lonely grief I sigh
For friends beloved, no longer nigh,
Submissive I would still reply—
　　　　　Thy will be done!

If thou should'st call me to resign
What most I prize, it ne'er was mine,
I only yield thee what was thine—
　　　　　Thy will be done!

If sickness wastes me to decay,
Let me with humble faith obey,
And teach thy servant still to pray—
　　　　　Thy will be done!

Renew my will from day to day,
Blend it with thine, and take away
All that now makes it hard to say—
　　　　　Thy will be done!

　　　　　　　　　　　BARBAULD.

FIAT VOLUNTAS.

Deus Pater, quando exulo
In asperis procul a domo,
Fac corde supplicem meo—
        Fiat voluntas O tua!

Sors ut siet mi tristior,
Ne murmurem superbior;
At vox sonet divinior,
        Fiat voluntas O tua!

Si raptum amicum defleam,
Solam tenens solus viam,
Fretus Deo respondeam—
        Fiat voluntas O tua!

Si me resignatum voces,
Quas arctius retineo res,
Nunquam meas—tuas habes;
        Fiat voluntas O tua!

Sin æger usque conterar,
Fidens humiliter obsequar,
Et des precanti ut eloquar—
        Fiat voluntas O tua!

Meam voluntatem nova,
Et indies misce tua;
Sitque petere arduum veta—
        Fiat voluntas O tua!

F. W.

RECOVERY FROM SICKNESS

O Saviour of the faithful dead,
  With whom thy servants dwell,
Though cold and green the turf is spread,
  Above their narrow cell;

No more we cling to mortal clay,
  We doubt and fear no more,
Nor shrink to tread the darksome way
  Which thou hast trod before.

'Twas hard from those I loved to go,
  Who knelt around my bed,
Whose tears bedewed my burning brow,
  Whose arms upheld my head!

As fading from my dizzy eyes,
  I sought their forms in vain,
The bitterness of death I knew,
  And groaned to live again.

'Twas dreadful when the accuser's power
  Assailed my sinking heart,
Recounting every wasted hour,
  And each unworthy part:

But, Jesus, in that mortal fray,
  Thy blessed comfort stole,
Like sunshine in a stormy day,
  Across my darkened soul.

IN VALETUDINEM REDITUS.

O MORTUORUM Tu fidelium salus,
    Quocum reviviscunt Tui,
Utcunque cespes frigidus lasciviat
    Super sepulcralem domum;

Non amplius complectimur mortalia,
    Effugit hæsitans metus;
Nec luridas timemus ire per vias,
    Quamque indicasti semitam.

Heu! quos amarem vix tuli relinquere,
    Circa torum stantes meum,
Frontem irrigantes aridam fletu pio,
    Caput levantes brachiis.

Vertiginosæ quum superstites mei
    Frustra petissent pupulæ,
Novi severam mortis expertus manum, et
    Ut parcerer, fudi preces.

Quis non inarsit horror in præcordiis,
    Quando imminens Vindex reo
Recensuit consumpta prave tempora,
    Et leviter effusos dies?

Sed dulce Christus adstitit solatium,
    In lite capitali mea;
Caliginoso sicut in die jubar,
    Animæ serenans nubila.

When soon or late this feeble breath
   No more to thee shall pray,
Support me through the vale of death,
   And in the darksome way.

When clothed in fleshly weeds again
   I wait thy dread decree,
Judge of the world, bethink thee then,
   That Thou hast died for me !

HEBER.

THE TEN COMMANDMENTS.

THOU shalt know no other gods but me,
Before no Idol bow thy knee.
Take not the name of God in vain,
Nor dare the Sabbath day profane.
Give both thy parents honour due,
Take heed that thou no murder do.
Abstain from words and deeds unclean,
Nor steal, though thou art poor and mean.
Nor tell a wilful lie, nor love it ;
What is thy neighbour's dare not covet.

WATTS.

Quocunque languens spiritus sub tempore
  Christum precari desinat,
In transeunda valle mortis adjuva,
  Manum in tenebris porrigens.

Cum carne rursus induar perterrita,
  Sententiam expectans gravem,
Sis o memor sis, Arbiter mortalium,
  Mihi morte vivendum Tua.

                                    H. D.

DECALOGUS.

Non aliud tibi Numen erit, Me præter : ad ullum
  Non cadet Idolon mensve genuve tuum :
Nullus abuteris divino Numine : nullus
  Sabbaticum audebis tu violare diem :
Semper honore suo donabis utrosque parentes :
  Vita alicui manibus ne sit adempta tuis :
Vocibus aut factis animum ne pollue pravis :
  Ne furare, licet nudus inopsque manes :
Nulla pati possis mendacia, dicere nulla :
  Et cave ne cupias, quas habet alter opes.

                                    F. H.

BALAAM'S PARABLE.

I shall see him, but not now:
I shall behold him, but not nigh:
There shall come a Star out of Jacob,
And a sceptre shall rise out of Israel,
And shall smite the corners of Moab,
And destroy all the children of Sheth.
And Edom shall be a possession,
Seir also shall be a possession for his enemies;
And Israel shall do valiantly.
Out of Jacob shall come he that shall have dominion,
And shall destroy him that remaineth in the city.
Amalek was the first of nations,
But his latter end shall be,
That he shall perish for ever.

NUMBERS XXIV.

EPITAPH.

Why should this earth delight us so?
    Why should we fix our eyes,
On these low grounds, were sorrows grow,
    And every pleasure dies?

CHURCHYARD POET.

VATES DEUM INTERPRETATUR.

Ego videbo! Ego aspiciam!
Ego illius novero faciem,
   Non nunc, at in posterum:
Stella de Jacob radios porriget,
Sceptrum in manibus Israel eriget
   In terrorem hostium!

Pellet a finibus hic Moabitam,
Eruet Shethi domum avitam,
   Cœlipotens Lacertus:
Ibit et Edomi satur spoliis,
Sheir et addet serti foliis,
   Israel ignea virtus.

Victor a Jacob mox dominabitur:
Neci quod superest urbium dabitur,
   Non immeritis vicibus:
Fuerit Amalek gentium gloria,
Illius illius cadet memoria
   Revulsa e radicibus!

H. D.

M. S.

Cur adeo nobis fugitiva hæc terra placebit?
  Cur oculos humili figimus usque solo?
Multus ubi exoritur dolor, accrescitque dolori;
  Et quicquid misero rideat orbe, perit?

F. H.

HEBREW MELODY.

THY days are done, thy fame begun;
　My country's strains record
The triumph of her chosen son,
　The slaughters of his sword;
The deeds he did, the fields he won,
　The freedom he restored!

Though thou art fallen, while we are free,
　Thou shalt not taste of death;
The generous blood that flows from thee
　Disdained to sink beneath:
Within our veins the current be,
　Thy spirit on our breath!

BYRON.

EVENING HYMN.

GOD, that madest earth and heaven,
　Darkness and light!
Who the day for toil hast given,
　For rest the night;
May thine angel guards defend us,
Slumber sweet thy mercy send us,
Holy dreams and hopes attend us
　This livelong night.

HEBER.

CARMEN HEBRAICUM.

Hæc famæ tibi prima dies, licet ultima vitæ :
 Vox patriæ laudes fert iterata tuas :
Illa canit, faciles quo duxeris orbe triumphos,
 Quot domitos socio straveris ense viros ;
Quas tuleris lauros, quos debellaveris hostes ;
 Quæ dederis populo libera jura tuo !

Sis licet abreptus, quædam pars grata manebit,
 Et, dum libertas nostra, perennis erit.
Corpore lapsa tuo generosi sanguinis unda
 Non tulit indignum commaculasse solum.
O nostræ tali turgescant flumine venæ,
 Vibret et in nostro spiritus ille sinu !

G. K.

HYMNUS VESPERTINUS.

O Deus, o Tu, qui terras cœlosque parasti,
 Quique diem et tenebras,
Qui perferre jubes læta sub luce labores,
 Otia nocte refers ;
Angelicis functos operum tueare ministris,
 Dum sopor altus habet ;
Spesque hilares adstent et longa noctis in hora
 Somnia sancta toris.

B.

AT A FUNERAL.

BENEATH our feet and o'er our head
  Is equal warning given,
Beneath us lie the countless dead,
  Above us is the heaven!

Their names are graven on the stone,
  Their bones are in the clay,
And ere another day is done,
  Ourselves may be as they.

Death rides on every passing breeze,
  He lurks in every flower,
Each season has its own disease,
  Its peril every hour.

Our eyes have seen the very light
  Of youth's soft cheek decay,
And fate descend in sudden night
  On manhood's middle day.

Our eyes have seen the steps of age
  Halt feebly towards the tomb,
And yet shall earth our hearts engage,
  And dreams of days to come?

Turn, mortal, turn! thy danger know;
  Where'er thy foot can tread,
The earth rings hollow from below,
  And warns thee of her dead.

IN EXSEQUIIS.

PAR est, quæ datur, monitio
Supra capita et infra pedes :
Supra, poli constitutio ;
Infra, mortuorum sedes !

Saxis constant scripta nomina,
Artus madida premit humus ;
Lux priusquam cessit crastina,
Quod sunt illi, forte nos sumus.

Mors Eurisque Zephyrisque
Equitat ; omni flore latet ;
Annus suis morbis, suisque
Quæque fatis hora scatet.

Vidimus roseum jubar genis
Marcescere mollis juventæ ;
Et vitæ ignibus in plenis
Descendere noctem repente.

Vidimus ægris graves annis
Eo vix ire, qua sit quies ;
Et carnis obsiti nos pannis
Multos somniamur dies ?

O vertere, mortalis homo !
Periculum qui nescit, cadit :
Terra de mortuorum domo
Cavum sonans, multa tradit.

Turn, Christian, turn ! thy soul apply
　　To truths divinely given ;
The bones that underneath thee lie
　　Shall live for hell or heaven !

HEBER.

THE END.

To die is landing on some silent shore,
Where billows never break nor tempests roar :
Ere well we feel the friendly stroke, 'tis o'er.
The wise, through thought, the insults of death defy,
The fools through blessed insensibility.
'Tis what the guilty fear, the pious crave,
Sought by the wretch, and vanquished by the brave ;
It eases lovers, sets the captive free,
And though a tyrant, offers liberty.

GARTH.

INTROIT.

Oh most merciful,
Oh most bountiful,
　　God the Father Almighty !
By the Redeemer's
Sweet intercession,
　　Hear us, hear us, when we cry !

HEBER.

O vertere, cui verba patent
Christi!—Cujus sis et eris :
Vivent, quæ subter ossa latent,
In superis aut in inferis.

H. D.

EXITUS ACTA PROBAT.

TALE mori, qualis placidam descensus in oram,
   Prævenit extremam mens ubi firma vicem.
Ingenio meliore suo Sapientia morti,
   Stultitia ingenio deteriore vacat.
Quam pravi timuere, pii optavere propinquam,
   Tristia quam quærunt, fortia corda domant ;
Vincula amatorum, captorum vincula solvit,
   Et præstat, quamvis dura magistra, fugam.

H. J. T. D.

INTROITUS.

O TU clementissime,
O tu benignissime,
   Qui rerum potens omnium,
Per gratiam Redimentis,
Per et Intercedentis,
   Audi, audi, vocantium !

H. D.

¹ Pæne in articulo mortis suæ redditum.

EPITAPH ON AN INFANT.

ERE sin could blight or sorrow fade,
  Death came with friendly care,
The opening bud to Heav'n conveyed,
  And bade it blossom there.

DONNE.

PSALM XXIII.

MY Shepherd is the living Lord,
  I therefore nothing need,
In pastures fair, near pleasant streams,
  He setteth me to feed.

He shall convert and glad my soul,
  And bring my mind in frame,
To walk in paths of righteousness,
  For His most holy name.

Yes, though I walk the vale of Death,
  Yet will I fear no ill;
Thy rod and staff they comfort me,
  And Thou art with me still.

And in the presence of my foes
  My table Thou hast spread,
Thou wilt fill full my cup, and Thou
  Anointed hast my head.

Through all my life Thy favour is
  So frankly shewn to me,
That in Thy house for evermore
  My dwelling place shall be.

OLD VERSION.

M. S.

ANTE malum quam te culpa maculaverat, ante
   Quam poterat primum carpere cura decus,
In cœlos gemmam leni mors transtulit ictu,
   Inque suo jussit sese aperire solo.

S. B.

PASTOR MEUS.

PASTOR meus, vivus Deus;
   Nihilo sum cariturus;
Pulcris pratis, aquis gratis,
   Ille me est aliturus.

Ducet viis Idem piis,
   Animam convertens meam;
Propter Nomen, felix omen
   Mihi dans, quocunque eam.

Mortis vallis, licet callis
   Fuerit, quo ambulabo;
At nil mali, fretus tali
   Certo Duce, formidabo.

Mensam cibis Tu parabis,
   Deus, hostes meos pungens;
Pocla mero Tu sincero
   Plena reddes, caput ungens.

Omnes rite dies vitæ
   Sic redundat Tua gratia;
Tu concedes, ut sint ædes
   Meæ in cœlis palatia.

H. D.

PRAYER FOR ABSOLUTION.

For every sentence, clause, and word,
That's not inlaid with thee, O Lord,
Forgive me, God! and blot each line
Out of my book, that is not thine—
But if midst all thou findest one
Wanting thy benediction,
That one of all the rest shall be
The glory of my work and me.

HERRICK.

PROPITIETUR DEUS.

Sı quid in his fuerit, sententia, clausula, verbum,
    Quod non te sapiat vel tua, sancte Deus,
O precor ignoscas, damnataque carmina dele ;
    Quodcunque· indignum vivere, dispereat.
Si tamen exciderit de tot modo versibus unus,
    Quem sinis æthereas, Maxime, adire domos,
Illud carmen erit, dum spiritus hos regit artus,
    Et vati et tremulæ gloria summa lyræ.

H. D.

AMHN.

For EU product safety concerns, contact us at Calle de José Abascal, 56–1°, 28003 Madrid, Spain or eugpsr@cambridge.org.

www.ingramcontent.com/pod-product-compliance
Ingram Content Group UK Ltd.
Pitfield, Milton Keynes, MK11 3LW, UK
UKHW010345140625
459647UK00010B/834